What's So Blessed About Being Poor?

What's So Blessed About Being Poor?

Seeking the Gospel in the Slums of Kenya

L. Susan Slavin and Coralis Salvador

ORBIS BOOKS

Maryknoll, New York 10545

Founded in 1970, Orbis Books endeavors to publish works that enlighten the mind, nourish the spirit, and challenge the conscience. The publishing arm of the Maryknoll Fathers and Brothers, Orbis seeks to explore the global dimensions of the Christian faith and mission, to invite dialogue with diverse cultures and religious traditions, and to serve the cause of reconciliation and peace. The books published reflect the views of their authors and do not represent the official position of the Maryknoll Society. To learn more about Maryknoll and Orbis Books, please visit our website atwww.maryknollsociety.org.

Library of Congress Cataloging-in-Publication Data

Slavin, L. Susan.
    What's so blessed about being poor? : seeking the Gospel in the slums of Kenya / L. Susan Slavin and Coralis Salvador.
        p. cm.
    ISBN 978-1-62698-055-6 (pbk.); ISBN 978-1-60833-324-8 (ebook)
    1. Missions—Kenya. 2. Church work with the poor. 3. Poverty—Religious aspects—Christianity. 4. Slavin, L. Susan. 5. Salvador, Coralis. I. Salvador, Coralis. II. Title.
BV3625.K4S54 2012
266'.26762--dc23

2012021119

*To the memory of Sister Dolores Fortier of the Missionary Sisters
of Our Lady of Africa, founder of the AIDS Orphans' Project
("I have come in order that you might have life—
life in all its fullness"
[John 10:10]);*

To the AIDS orphans, their grandmothers, and guardians; and

To our beloved children and grandchildren.

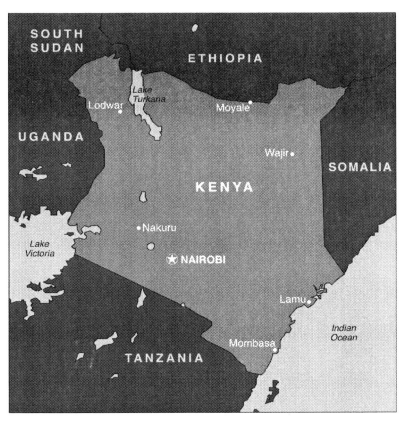

Map of Kenya

Contents

Acknowledgments

As with any idea for a book, especially among novice authors, the initial concept comes far easier than its implementation. What began as a theological debate between us materialized into a *heavy and dense* submission for publication that was understandably rejected.

We were always encouraged, however, that the story of the orphans was a good story and to just tell it. That brought us to the winter of 2011 when both of us secluded ourselves in Susan's home in New York to rewrite the manuscript. Incredibly, into our lives came Ryan Vollmer, Susan's neighbor and friend. Intrigued by the story, Ryan offered to assist in editing. Throughout six snowy, cold, blizzard-laden weeks, we wrote, rewrote, and e-mailed the text next door to Ryan as she edited, cut, questioned, prodded, and literally forced us to just tell the story. Ryan's selflessness in supporting this endeavor is without reservation and our gratitude to her is unbounded.

In addition to our families, there are many friends and colleagues who encouraged us. We owe special recognition to our readers—those who plowed through various drafts and offered comments and criticisms. Thank you to Sister Eileen Hauswald, OSF, Rhegan Hyypio, Russ Brine, Eva Murray Scelzo, Mary Oldham, Judith Beckman, Carol Markman, Dinggay la O', Brenda Montera, Lynne Cohen, and Salvatore Trifiletti.

Susan Perry, our editor, has been a most patient counselor. She saw the possibilities from the early days and guided the text from what was a heavy and dense academic, lawyerly like brief, filled with footnotes, to a story of hope, certitude, and joy. To Sue, the Franciscan blessing of "Peace and all good" goes along with our gratitude.

Introduction

March 12, 2010, Nairobi, Kenya

In one sense we are always traveling, and traveling as if we do not know where we are going. In another sense we have already arrived. We cannot arrive at the perfect possession of God in this life, and that is why we are traveling in the darkness. But we already possess God by grace, and therefore in that sense we have arrived and are dwelling in the light. But, oh! How far have I to go to find you in whom I have already arrived?[1]

We were walking very briskly through Kibera, a slum in Nairobi, Kenya, on a Friday in March of 2010. There were no roads, only dirty, dusty, rocky paths twisting and turning in one direction or another through a jigsaw maze of twig and mud shanties. The air was heavy with the stench of humanity mingled with the odor of outdoor charcoal cooking fires. I was not looking where I was going. Instead I was looking down, dodging brown streams of urine and excrement oozing from plastic bags. I was also trying to avoid the

---

[1] Thomas Merton, *The Seven Storey Mountain* (New York: Harcourt Brace, 1948), 458–59.

The Kibera slums in Nairobi, one of the largest in Africa,
where one million people live.

myriad small piles of burning garbage. I remember thinking, thank God I'd worn sneakers and not sandals, since the thought of human waste between my bare toes simply grossed me out. I expected a certain amount of physical discomfort with mission work, but I drew the line at walking through human waste with open sandals.

In Kibera thousands of people of all shapes and sizes were living in unfathomable conditions, stripped of human dignity and living life on the margins—an impossible situation for Westerners to comprehend. Children called out "*mzungu*" (foreigner or white person) and "Howareyou?" in an attempt to beg.

I couldn't remember the Swahili phrase I was told to say—words that weren't an outright rejection, but rather something like "not today," a phrase that would deny their request but still give them some hope. Would I ever see these street children again? How could I ever give hope to these kids whom many consider disposable? And yet I witnessed brief touching moments of unexpected human dignity. Some people, on their way to work, were dressed in immaculately pressed shirts and pants. How was it possible to iron clothes without electricity? Later I learned that they did it the old-fashioned way with heavy irons heated on cooking fires.

No one unfamiliar with Kibera, be it Kenyan or Westerner, walks through its alleys and narrow streets alone. Coralis Salvador and I were blindly following a very experienced missionary leader who was walking through at a very rapid pace, weaving us in and out of this congested maze. I'd first met Coralis in the fall of 2006 when I was a volunteer lawyer teaching human rights as part of a Justice and Peace program on the Kenyan coast. Back then, Coralis met me at the Mombasa airport in southern Kenya after a long and arduous journey traveling from New York to London to Nairobi and finally south to Mombasa. I was very glad to be taken under her wing. During those first few days I not only suffered from extreme jet lag, I was emotionally and physically stunned by the human degradation and poverty. But Coralis and I became fast friends and kept in close contact over the years.

As I received her quarterly reports in the years since our first meeting in 2006, I became fascinated by her story of the AIDS Orphans' Project in Mombasa, a coastal region of Kenya that has one of the highest concentrations of AIDS orphans in Africa. This project had consumed the last ten years of Coralis's life. In our many communications over the ensuing years, including two return trips to Kenya for me, Coralis told me about the undoubting hope and faith of the AIDS orphans amidst all this despair and misery. Hearing her describe the orphans and her work with them brought the Beatitudes to my mind, especially that well-known phrase, "blessed are the poor." I was incredibly skeptical. How could the marginalized poor, seemingly stripped of human dignity, these people I'd seen on a number of trips to Nicaragua and now Kenya, be blessed? Where, and how, living as they were, could they be blessed?

You see, I recognize that Coralis is a true believer, and I greatly respect both her spirituality and her intellect. Her way of being in the world is to see God's hand in most everything, including the minutiae. When she would articulate her spirituality, I would generally offer a quick contrary retort, something along the lines of "God doesn't micromanage this or that." Coralis would then just give me a knowing smile or a nod of her head, implying something like "foolish Susan." When we first met in 2006, I was something of a cynic, filled with faith yet a "cafeteria Catholic" who constantly railed against the institutional church, primarily on the issue of women's rights. Over the years, however, Coralis taught me to be compassionate yet realistic, and she remains the only person I have met who articulates a theology and spirituality that makes sense to me.

On this particular day in March 2010 we had traveled from her home in Mombasa to Nairobi to meet two of the AIDS orphans who were among some of the first young people to make it to the university. The AIDS program that Coralis helps run finds guardians for the orphans, in addition to securing their primary and sometimes secondary education.

After my first contact with Coralis in 2006, I wanted to understand how someone could be both very poor and yet blessed. I had approached it as a lawyer would, by doing research in books. I exhausted the materials in the public libraries of Long Island, New York, where I live. Then I obtained library privileges at a theological library, but I still didn't find any answers. I sent my research to Coralis for her comments. Her experiences as a missioner, someone who daily touches the suffering of the poor, were in no way reflected in my research. We argued time and again via Skype and e-mail. Coralis challenged me to "put down the books and come and see" for myself, so I did. When I returned to Kenya in March of 2010, I interviewed AIDS orphans, young adults, and teens, those who were currently enrolled in the program and those who had completed it. I talked to social workers, nurses, community workers, and missioners. I challenged and prodded and was very much an "in your face Westerner" (and a New York litigator!!).

This is the story of what I learned. It is a story of hope, faith, spirit, dignity, and determination. It is the story of the search for an answer to the question of what Jesus means in the beatitude in Luke's gospel: "blessed are the poor" (Luke 6:20). I slowly found my answer within the context of the ten-year history of the AIDS Orphans' Project in Mombasa.

Whether Muslim or Christian, incredibly, the orphans said that God was there for them, "every day, because we breathe, we walk, we see the day . . . then we are OK." The young adults told me that being "poor but hardworking" or "poor but determined" or "poor but truthful" were their blessings. The social workers, health-care workers, and others whose mission is to minister to the poor articulated other blessings such as being "poor with spirit" or "poor with dignity." However, they also said that the blessings were not a free pass to sit passively with one's hand stretched out for help. The blessing was not for those who made poverty their *job*. But what is the blessing?

There is no more challenging or better place to explore the possible answer than Kenya, a developing country that has a relatively low incidence of AIDS compared to other countries on the African continent, although HIV/AIDS is always most prevalant among the poor. It is estimated that between 25 and 30 percent of the inhabitants of slums like Kibera and those in Mombasa are HIV positive, and an astonishing two-thirds of the children under the age of eighteen are HIV positive. Many of Kibera's approximately one million residents are unemployed. Those who manage to find work generally earn less than one dollar per day selling fruits and vegetables or working as unskilled laborers. Although Kibera accounts for less than 1 percent of Nairobi's total area, it holds more than one-quarter of its population. At present the greatest challenge to the people infected by AIDS is not a lack of effective drugs but a lack of food. Shockingly, quite a few AIDS victims die from starvation rather than illness. The Kenyan government does not officially recognize Kibera or other such slums, and they do not exist on any official maps. Because the inhabitants receive no services, such as water, electricity, sewage, schools, or medical facilities, structural injustices and institutional sin abound.

As we walked along a railroad track in Kibera that day in March, I assumed it was abandoned because I couldn't imagine how a train could pass through this area. Squeezed right up next to the tracks were hundreds of one-room shanties, cooking stands the size of old-time telephone booths, and mounds of burning garbage. There wasn't an inch to spare, but, in fact, trains pass along this track five times per day. Forget about safety—there are no platforms, no rails, no gates, no advance warnings of any kind. Personal injury lawyers in New York would have a field day litigating all the accidents and wrongful deaths in this tort heaven.

We quickly weaved in and out of crowded ramshackle structures haphazardly sandwiched together in abysmal density. When I once dared to look up, I noticed a wooden stall jammed into the corner of an interior market. On the outside of the stall, in large pink letters, were the words "Cho 5 shillings" (about seven cents). It was an outhouse that costs about three cents to use. I concluded that was better than being struck by one of the "flying toilets," human waste deposited in plastic bags and tossed wherever, which was the usual way people relieved themselves.

We were headed for the John Paul II Secondary Vocational School, which teaches carpentry and cement work to boys and sewing to girls. The school's library—the first ever in Kibera—was a crowning achievement for the community. We climbed a circular staircase in a real building that housed administrative offices. The walls were covered with a stunning two-story African mural painted by local artists. It was illuminated by brilliant light that poured in from oversized windows overlooking a panoramic view of Kibera. The open, clean, quiet, and reflective library was a striking contrast to the bleak, gray humanity outside its doors. The students, dressed in dusty crimson shorts and jumpers, played outside in an open yard and ran up to us screaming a delighted sing-song "howareyou." The smaller children mobbed us, so many wanting to touch the *wazungu*.

We were then led into a stunning circular church that would look right at home on the north shore of Long Island. At Christ the King we took tea in the priest's house, which had running water, a flush toilet, and electricity, and was surrounded by a path and garden lush with bright flowering plants and shrubs. I was struck by the contrast between the beautiful vegetation and the slum that was veiled in murky, muted browns and grays. Amazingly the church was funded by the people of Kibera. Father Peter, one of the Irish Kiltegan priests stationed there, calmly told us that within the next five years his order was leaving, since the people of Kibera would be independent and no longer need them. That seemed hard to believe in a place where the government was rife with corruption and greed.

My curiosity would have to wait because we were in a hurry to leave Kibera. That's how it is there; you're always in a hurry, and for safety's sake you walk with a determined purpose. I was deep in thought, wondering why I was even in Kibera. My camera was tucked away because I didn't want to take any photos; it felt disrespectful, like gawking: "Hey, do you want to see my photos of the poor people living in wretched conditions?" Also, an expensive camera is likely to be plucked right out from your hands.

We met with a Justice and Peace social worker in Kibera's Office of Human Rights. We made our way up the stairs to a makeshift office made out of used wood and exposed nails with old computers wedged in wherever there was space. I had worked with the Justice and Peace group within the Office of Human Rights in 2006, traveling with a very experienced field worker to villages along the Mombasa coast. The goal of the program was to inform the people of their human rights regarding AIDS, rape, and many other issues, as well as to implore them to get tested for AIDS. Surely, I thought, Nairobi's Justice and Peace activities would be more advanced than those in Mombasa, but I quickly learned not to jump to conclusions.

Human rights abuses are rampant in Kibera. In addition to the sickness, diseases, and all of the injustices associated with wretched poverty, the postelection violence of the Kenyan national election in 2007/2008 witnessed competing tribes looting, burning, raping, and murdering their African brothers and sisters. Within this seeming negation of humanity, the social workers actually have to pay people to get them to come to meetings to learn about their rights according to the new constitution voted into effect in 2010, shortly after I arrived. Having to pay people to gain information that will benefit them sounds outlandish, but it was the only way to (hopefully) lift them out of illiteracy and degradation.

As a result of the staggering number of rapes that occurred as part of the postelection violence and continued through the fragile peace, the Justice and Peace workers held an educational rape session, again paying the women to attend and also offering them lunch and two tea breaks. The women learned what to do if they were raped: they were not to bathe, and they were to go immediately to a clinic. They were reassured that as victims they would be treated with dignity; the police would be alerted; and, hopefully, the rapist would be arrested. After reviewing all the information, the social worker asked the women what they should do if they were raped. To her dismay, the overwhelming response was "Ask the chief!" The social worker was stunned. Despite all they had learned, the women fell back on tribal customs, an ancient system deeply entrenched in every facet of African life and not likely to change overnight.

As I continued my journey after my visit to the Office of Human Rights, I started across the railroad track. I was startled by a very loud train horn. I looked up and saw a big, black, fast-moving train barreling down on me. I screamed and jumped back. As I attempted to recover from that near-death experience, I yelled back to Coralis, "Did you see that? DID YOU SEE THAT?!!!!!" She said "*Pole*" ("sorry" in Swahili) *Pole*???? Before I had left home I made sure all my affairs were in order, but I wasn't ready for all those plans to be put into effect by one stupid, careless, *mzungu* crossing the railroad track!

Incredibly hot, uncomfortable, and frightened, I immediately questioned whether I was cut out for all this acculturation. I started thinking about my very comfortable life as a New York attorney and my own evolving spirituality. Intellectually I knew that a missioner signs up for living in a mystery and is required to give up certainty and control.

I also knew that I was undergoing a conversion of sorts. I was leaving my position of privilege and moving toward the margins of society. And through it all, my motivations were driven by seeking an answer to the question of Where is God in the middle of all this and what's so damn blessed about being poor?

While all the reading I had done taught me little, Coralis and her orphans provided me with an answer. Coralis Salvador, a lay missionary, left her comfortable California home and family to dance in closer union with her love, her Lord, and her God. She had been called to the vocation of missioner, to become an agent of change, and to take on a deeper interior life so that she would be able to pass the fruits of her contemplation on to others. She exposed and articulated her beliefs and demonstrated to me and many others her humanity and developing faith, with all its permutations and dents. Coralis was surely not alone.

The story of Coralis and of other missioners and Justice and Peace workers throughout the world speaks of an extreme and profound paradox. They have come to know people who live in wretched inhumanity and who suffer greatly and yet who have a sense of joy and hope at the center of their being. As I tell the story of Coralis and her missionary work with AIDS orphans, I'm also telling the story of many others. It is the story also of those who mentored her: healthcare workers, social workers, guardians, volunteers, and other missioners—Christians and Muslims alike.

Coralis's story tells about her work and the pain, the joy, the sorrow, and the dehumanization of the poor in Kenya. Her story also demonstrates with clarity her own spirituality, her way of being in the world with God. I entered into her story as a cynic, ready to challenge not only her beliefs, but also those of the orphans and health-care and social workers as well as her fellow missioners. This is their story, but along the way it led me to a spirituality I was not even aware existed. And it became my story as I decided to join Coralis in her work and began a program of formation with the Franciscan Mission Service to become a lay missionary in Africa.

Chapter 1

"Mama Coralis" Salvador, August 2008

Mama Coralis is sitting in her office in Changamwe, an industrial area of Mombasa located on the mainland. This is a busy time for the AIDS orphans, especially the older children who are in high school. They are lined up waiting to meet with Coralis, one-on-one, to review their end of the year grades. Everyone is anxious and tense. A high-school education is a way out of crushing poverty for each of them and for their extended families. If they don't keep their grades up, Coralis will have to make the gut-wrenching, Solomonistic decision to drop them from the program and give their place to someone else, and the waiting list is already long. There is simply too much need and not enough money to educate all the deserving children. The Kenyan government, like many in the impoverished Global South, does not provide free secondary education to its citizens. As a result, many nongovernmental agencies (NGOs) have filled the vacuum in an effort to provide education and thus hope, especially for the orphans and the families that have taken them in after their parents have died from AIDS. Coralis places the children in a variety of public schools, probably more than twenty in number, which are nondenominational. Since the project cannot supply transportation, the orphans are placed in the schools nearest their homes.

For eight years Coralis has lived among people who, by circumstance of birth in a developing country, experience unimaginable hardship. She absolutely loves her work, including the daily routine of driving or taking a *matatu* from Mombasa, the second largest Kenyan city and a large port on the Indian Ocean, to her office in Changamwe. *Matatus* are actually minivans, akin to the VW vans so popular in the 1960s. They are also brightly painted on the outside, usually with praise to Allah and/or Christ. Music blasts out from speakers on the inside and on top of the van. The sound is deafening and is accompanied by loud, incessant horn honking. The music blasting from speakers on top of the *matatus* may be from Bob Marley or songs to Allah or gospel songs. The main road, the Makupa Causeway, connecting the island of Mombasa to the mainland, is clogged both day and night with huge container trucks, *matatus*, cars, and push carts piled high with everything from vegetables, fruits, or charcoal to whatever else needs to be transported from Kongowea to Changamwe. There are no sidewalks, no traffic lights, no police, just a mass of children, adults, and random goats and chickens. The causeway is lined with one-story wooden shops of every kind and ramshackle cement structures.

Every day on her way to work Coralis passes a towering dump of burning garbage on the side of the road where the rats have burrowed into every available crevice. In the beginning she was overwhelmed by the stench, but she has gotten used to it. Then on a hillside, as far as the eye can see, is the Kibarani slum, a former garbage dump, where approximately 100,000 people now live in mud huts with thatched roofs or sometimes just plastic sheets for the roof. A number of Coralis's AIDS orphans live in the

Kibarani slum where families pay about four to six dollars per month for rent. As in the Kibera slum in Nairobi, the Kenyan government provides no services whatsoever: no water, no electricity, no sewerage. Residents buy their water from men who illegally tap into the main water pipes of the city, filling their beat-up, yellow jerry cans and pushing their valuable cargo, bumping and grunting, up and down through the slum's muddy paths. The closest primary school is Tudor, which is located outside the slum, and the children must walk about forty-five minutes each way and cross a main road to reach it.

Coralis alights from the *matatu* and walks for a mile or so to her office in St. Mary's Parish compound. The road twists and turns, and huge potholes the size of push carts abound, along with assorted garbage, goats, and chickens. Fine dust gets into everything. In the rainy season, people jump from one small patch of dry land to another to reach their destination. It seems like a giant flea market: every-where people are selling things—tires, chains, metals, spare engine parts, bikes, used clothing, fruits and vegetables. While the women usually sell food, men sell everything else. Gender roles are strictly adhered to throughout most of Kenya. The village chief's office is prominently located to the left of the first bend in the dirt road. Coralis has a very positive relationship with him, and he often brings bags of food to Coralis for her orphans. Coralis loves the walk because she never knows whom she will meet along the way. She also never knows what she will be walking in along the road—sometimes raw sewage—but generally not the human waste she frequently encounters in Kibera. She is constantly greeted by joyful adults and children. She feels loved by the children, and she in turn loves them.

Coralis spends about three days in the main office in Changamwe and two other days in the Mikindani Voluntary Counseling and Testing Clinic (VCT). She shares office space with Marion, the community-based health-care nurse who provides the HIV-positive clients with health-care, testing, and counseling. Illness permeates the air of the clinic. New patients, gaunt and weak, arrive regularly, usually accompanied by a health-care worker. Many more of the AIDS patients are women than men because generally the men won't seek help, and so they are dying younger and faster than the women. They are often in denial until almost the end of their disease, even though help is available.

*   *   *

Esha Abdallah is sitting on a long bench in the corridor with the other high-school students as well as some AIDS patients. When it's her turn, she enters Coralis's office with her head down, her speech barely audible. She is seventeen, a little older than the average high-school student. By nature a reserved young woman, she is a serious student who shows great promise. She wants to be a lawyer. Although generally quiet, she is quite articulate. She is wearing glasses and an off-white *hijab*, a veil that comes down below her waist, over a light gray skirt, a light blue shirt with the crest of the school on the breast pocket, a grey necktie, and long white cotton pants. Esha's only visible skin, light brown in color, is the oval cut out of her face and her lower arms. Her attire is that of a practicing Muslim.

Esha's parents both died of AIDS when she was quite young and her maternal aunt, Winnie, became her guardian. Winnie converted to Islam when she married, and her family strictly adheres to Muslim customs. She insisted that Esha

Seventeen-year-old Esha Abdallah,
who wanted to become a lawyer.

become a Muslim and dress like a proper Muslim woman. In addition to Esha, Winnie is raising her own six children as well as several other nephews and nieces.

Esha closes the door and hands her report card to Coralis. She looks ashamed; her grades are poor, barely passing. Coralis is shocked since for the past two years her grades have been great. "What happened?" Coralis blurts out as she scans the document. "What happened? Why did your grades go down? This is not you, what is the problem?" Coralis knows immediately something is amiss. This girl is known as the silent bookworm and is always reading. At first her words come out slowly, then in a big gush she says, "I moved out of my Aunt Winnie's house. I have dreams, night after night, of my dead mother." In the dreams her mother tells her to take on the Catholic faith and be baptized since she is from a Catholic family. Esha was never baptized because her parents died when she was so young. Her aunt, however, would not even hear of Esha converting to Catholicism. When Winnie became Esha's guardian, she became, in essence, her mother, thus automatically making Esha Muslim. Although Esha is a sensitive person who wants to obey her elders, she is deeply conflicted. Unable to withstand the pressure, at the beginning of the semester she has moved in with another aunt from her Catholic mother's side of the family. Winnie disagreed with her decision to leave. Esha is devastated, and her pain is palpable. She is caught between two worlds—two families and two faith traditions—in a seemingly irreconcilable conflict.

Esha's plight is both cultural and religious. In the African culture, Muslim practices are strongly enforced. When she tried to remove her veil in school, which was predominately Muslim, she was challenged by her teachers and the headmaster: "Why are you not wearing your *hijab*?" How could she explain what she herself didn't really understand? Coralis feels like a mother to Esha, and Esha has been in her program for six years. Herself a mother of five, Coralis understands that Esha loves her Aunt Winnie, even while she is haunted by dreams of her mother who wants her to go back to her birth faith. Coralis is not surprised that Esha's grades are failing. Nonetheless, there is a long line of AIDS orphans waiting for funds for secondary school. If a student is not performing well, he or she is usually given the option of going to a vocational school. In this particular case, though, Coralis won't give up on Esha.

Coralis touches Esha's hand and embraces her. "This is not the time to be baptized, Esha," she says. "God knows that in your heart you are baptized by your desire to be a Catholic. Wait until you are eighteen and you will be an adult. Right now it is your responsibility to finish your education with good marks, so you can get a scholarship and go to college to become a lawyer. God understands what you want, but you can't do it on your own, and you need your Aunt Winnie right now. Finish high school and then you will have the tools to go out on your own." Thankfully, Esha is able to put her crisis on hold. She goes back to live with Aunt Winnie, and her grades improve somewhat, but she never gets back to being a top student. She doesn't score well enough in the national examination to qualify for the university. Esha is very disappointed in herself and also in disappointing Coralis. Instead of going to the university, she enrolls in computer courses.

Over the next few months, Esha stops by Coralis's office to say hello. Outwardly Esha appears to have overcome her angst of the previous year. A few weeks later

Coralis is getting ready for a much anticipated Education for Life program, a three-day workshop for about one hundred of the orphans that includes ethnic food, team-building activities, and empowerment sessions on issues such as children's rights and drugs. Just before the program begins, Coralis is called out into the hall by one of Esha's cousins, a fourteen-year-old boy. In a very matter of fact way, with no emotion, the boy tells Coralis that Esha will not be attending the workshop because she died two days earlier. Gasping, Coralis asks what happened. Unbeknown to anyone, Esha was pregnant and gave birth to a baby girl the previous week in her aunt's home, on a mat on the floor, attended by a midwife. The baby survived, but after a week of hemorrhaging, Esha was finally brought to the hospital where she died. She was too weak to ever hold her baby.

Coralis is devastated. She cries for Esha as she embraces the boy. "This is a big loss," she says. "I feel guilty that I was not there for her. I did not know she was pregnant. Why didn't she tell me? I could have helped her, and there are doctors available. There was no reason for her to die." Coralis also feels betrayed by Esha. She felt she had a genuine connection with her and that Esha would willingly confide in her. But Esha didn't tell anyone; she bore this all alone. For one of the first and few times in her nearly ten years as a missioner in Kenya, Coralis questions God. "How could this be?" Winnie will now be saddled with taking care of this baby whom she can ill afford. Esha, who yearned for parental love, had now left an orphan—the orphan of an orphan. This cruel cycle repeats itself again and again. When will it end, Lord? Where is the justice for the wretched poor?

Winnie has been a good guardian, a caring guardian. She is a very hard worker who has participated in a micro-lending program that has enabled her to sell *chapati*, a flat bread, and boiled beans from a rented room that she lives in with her family. This includes six of her own children, four nephews and nieces, and now Esha's baby.

Shortly after Esha's death, Winnie comes to see Coralis. They embrace in silence and Coralis whispers "*Pole*" (sorry) to Winnie. *Pole* for the death of Esha*, pole* for the newborn who was now left motherless, and *pole* for Coralis who feels the crushing burden of not doing enough for Esha. Coralis sobs for this young life, full of hope, who dealt with her over-whelming secret alone. She sobs for the baby who will never know her mother. Esha had yearned for parental love and now so would her daughter. In that tearful embrace, Winnie tells Coralis that right before she died, Esha spoke to her and said, "Mama, I am dying." Winnie gave her permission for Esha to be buried in the Catholic rite. This is a small com-fort for Coralis, but she is pleased that Winnie respects Esha's wishes. Coralis knows that Winnie's heart is big and that she will do her best to take good care of the baby.

Where is God in this tragedy? "This is in God's hands," Coralis tells Winnie. "God is in every event, God is nev-er absent, or I would have collapsed already and not have had the strength to continue. God is not absent, and even though I cannot understand what is happening, there is a bigger picture. There is something, but I cannot see it at this moment." Coralis offers Winnie the opportunity to place the child in an orphanage in the hope of a future adoption, but Winnie declines. She will raise the child. More than ever, Coralis clings to her God, assured in the belief that everything is a gift from God, including the hurt and the

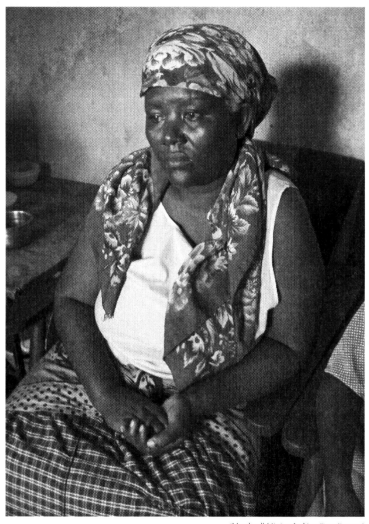

Aunt Winnie Wamboi.

joy. That is the unending paradox in this mystery. "God is there for us but not just in the good things."

Like so many Kenyan women, Winnie is very strong. Even so, Coralis wonders why no one in the family reached out for help when Esha lay bleeding on the mat on the floor. Was it the shame of the birth in the first place? Was it the condemnation of fellow Muslims? Or was it simply the Kenyan way—we do what we can and do not ask for help if we ourselves can take care of the situation. Indeed, Esha's death is a simple fact, a part of life, the Kenyan way. Is this a blessing of the poor? Here tragedy is not separate; it's simply a normal part of life just as the ancestors who have died are still a part of life. Winnie will continue to carry the burden of this tragedy, but she is blessed because God is keeping her strong. She remains totally composed and dignified. Winnie regards this child, like any other newborn, as a blessing. Even though Winnie hoped that Esha, once educated, would help carry the family's burdens, now she is gone, leaving behind a small newborn burden.

Reflecting on this tragedy, Coralis remains steadfast in her faith. "The Lord stretches us, in many different situations, to pour out love even though it's going to hurt, even though it's going to put us out of our comfort zone. That's what the love of God is. Winnie is a big-hearted woman who sees this new child as a blessing." Then Coralis addressed me: "Susan, you've been asking 'What's so blessed about being poor?' But aren't you now more aware of God in your life, mentally and spiritually? Aren't you more aware of the grace of God, even though you don't know what grace is."

Coralis is envious of Winnie's strength. As they embrace, Winnie is consoling Coralis instead of the other way around. And where is Esha's blessing in this tragedy? She always wanted parental love, and Winnie gave her that love, showing it especially in her choice of burial rites. Esha brought forth life, a new beginning, a flower blooming full of hope. Why did she die? We simply do not know.

Chapter 2

Blessed Are Those
Who Are Poor but Determined

The story of Exodus is the great story of liberation that gave hope to the enslaved people of Egypt. God said to Moses, "I have seen the misery of my people. . . . I have heard their cry. . . . I know their suffering and I have come to deliver them" (Exodus 3:7–8). In ancient Israel, poverty was seen as an egregious injustice. That God chose to recognize the plight of the Hebrew people, his created beings, from the onset of the covenant is a consistent theme that permeates the Hebrew Scriptures. It is this theme that forms the basis of Christ's ministry on Earth.

Coralis Salvador began her spiritual journey into the wilderness in her native Philippines. Divorced, she moved her five children to San Francisco in 1983. A lover of dance from an early age, as she matured spiritually she envisioned dance as a metaphor for her life and wondered where the next dance would lead her when her children were grown. "I asked the Lord what he wanted me to do with this second act of my life," she says. "I wanted to dance with the Lord, to be in rhythm with Jesus. Like the story of Exodus, I knew of the suffering people in the heart of Africa and I wanted to be present to them. I had faith and a true conviction that God is good to humanity but didn't understand how this could be reconciled with the suffering poor." Yet

Coralis knew instinctively that if she listened to the Lord, the very epitome of goodness and truth, he would liberate her and lead her where she should be.

Theologian Albert Nolan describes this compassion as the basis of truth.

> The experience of compassion is the experience of suffering or feeling with someone. To suffer or feel with humanity, nature and God is to be in tune with the rhythms and impulses of life. This is also the experience of solidarity, solidarity with humanity, nature and God.[1]

Coralis believed that God was an encounter to meet and act upon, and this informed the basis of her life. There was no longer an *I*, a *me*, or *myself*, but rather a desire to be absorbed in God's presence.

*   *   *

In San Francisco Coralis had worked as a bank administrator. She was also active in her local parish and the Filipino community, and she was a volunteer for the local HIV/ AIDS suicide nightline. She also practiced "centering prayer," a method of silent prayer that prepares the person to open oneself to God's presence. Such an approach emphasizes prayer as a personal relationship with God. Yet Coralis knew that something was missing in her life. "I knew that God was at the center of everything, but I felt unconnected and yearned to expand outside of what I call my selfish interior. I permitted myself to be led into the unknown. My faith enabled me to take the hand of the one who was leading

---

[1] Albert Nolan, *Jesus before Christianity* (Maryknoll, NY: Orbis Books, 1992), 152.

me, knowing full well that the family I left behind would be cared for by the Lord." Coralis was confident that her faith would sustain her in whatever was to come, and she trusted it would be good for her. The search for the reign of God called her, and she was absolutely certain that she would find it in relationship with the lives of the poor of Africa.

How Does a Person Become a Missioner?

Coralis went to Africa to satisfy an inner thirst for a closer union with God. She firmly believed she could not attain that union by remaining in the comfort of her life in San Francisco. Henri Nouwen, a theologian of spirituality, tells us,

> Jesus does not look at the events of our times as a series of incidents and accidents that have little to do with us. Jesus sees the political, economic and social events of our life as signs that call for a spiritual in-terpretation. They need to be read spiritually! But how? Jesus shows us how. . . . He says "What happened invites you to conversion!" This is the deepest meaning of history: a constant invitation calling us to turn our hearts to God and so discover the full meaning of our lives.[2]

Coralis believes that this call to conversion is not reflec-tive of any single organized religion. True conversion goes beyond the arbitrary boundaries of institutional religious training. It seeks to build a deeper relationship with God. It affects the spiritual dimension in each of our lives, which is

---

[2] Henri Nouwen, *Jesus: A Gospel*, ed. Michael O'Laughlin (Maryknoll, NY: Orbis Books, 2001), 59–60.

given to us by God. It is the Divine who challenges us to explore this other dimension of our being.

In August 2000 Coralis joined the Maryknoll Lay Missioners. She chose Maryknoll because it was familiar as she had graduated from Maryknoll College in the Philippines. She entered the training program in Ossining, New York, and took numerous classes in spirituality, missiology, and scripture, as well as the practical classes needed to understand mission. She most enjoyed classes that focused on living and working in a foreign culture. After four months of training, she arrived in Africa in January 2001 and then spent five months in language school to learn basic Swahili.

Once in Nairobi, the capital city of Kenya, the call to be a voice for the voiceless most assuredly began to deepen and strengthen within her as she witnessed firsthand the wretched world of the truly poor. "No amount of training could prepare me for the culture shock I encountered when I first arrived in Nairobi," she says. "The reality of life in Nairobi was simply too difficult to absorb. The vast majority of the people live in wretched slums, and the chaos of the city and its total neglect by the government seemed beyond comprehension. Initially, I was paralyzed with fear and wanted to run home to California, but I forced myself to conquer my fear just like I had done so many times in the past." She decided to address her fear directly in much the same way as advised by Henri Nouwen:

> Jesus speaks to us in the Gospel with very strong words. Throughout the Gospel, we hear "Do not be afraid. . . ." Fear is not of God, I am the God of love, a God who invites you to receive, to receive the gifts

of joy and peace and gratitude of the poor, and to let
go of your fears so that you can start sharing what
you are so afraid to let go of.[3]

In June 2001 Coralis arrived for a month of language
practice in Mombasa, located southeast of Nairobi, on the
coast of the Indian Ocean. For Maryknollers, language
practice is very much a hands-on approach. She practiced
her Swahili among the people instead of in the classroom.
Having seemingly overcome her initial shock, she hoped
that she would eventually learn to view the unknown in
a different light. Physically petite, she was always attired in
bright colors seemingly coordinated to go with the traditional Kenyan *kanga*, the intricately designed African cloth
women wear over their clothes from the waist down and as
head scarves. She wore an ever-present matching necker-
chief to accommodate the brutal African heat, and lipstick
and makeup were the order of the day. Her attire was in
striking contrast to the Muslim women completely covered
and veiled in black. She also learned to drive on the left
side of the road in a city with no more than four traffic
lights, with very few police directing traffic, and a constant
barrage of vendor push carts and street children weaving in
and out of traffic. In time, she became an incredibly aggres-
sive driver even by New York City standards!

Coralis soon began to immerse herself in the East African way of living and thinking. It was not long before
the Kenyan way of life eventually gave her the courage to
manage her own life while living in solidarity with Kenyans. However, she had to constantly remind herself that
she was not there to change anything or anyone based on her

---

[3] Ibid., 57–58.

personal agenda. That was not her calling. Her goal was to share her Christian experience in the hope that something good would eventually come out of it. In the decade that followed, through the lives of the poor, those afflicted with AIDS, and their families, she learned to live on the edge of the reign of God knowing that God is present, absolutely, everywhere, to everyone. "Since we all are part of the mystical body of Jesus Christ, the motivation of my mission was to bring those I ministered to into that body. At the same time, I had to respect the faith beliefs and ideas of the people I served. I was transformed into a totally different missioner. I learned to be present to the events and people and to be in union with God."

The Injustice of Poverty in the Hebrew Scriptures

The psalms in the Hebrew Scriptures are a collection of individual prayers, songs of lament, and expressions of praise by the chosen people of God. The psalms excoriate the rich and give hope to the poor. In the context of the Hebrew Scriptures, *poor* and *poverty* refer to actual material hunger, the lack of food and shelter, and all the social and personal tragedies associated with such a situation. This state of mental and physical suffering is an injustice, and thus the people cried out to the God of Israel whom they knew was not detached. His devotion and mercy are specifically directed toward the poor whom God shields with compassion. To rectify this injustice, the Israelites believed that a Messiah would eventually come and liberate the poor. There was a sense of hope for a reversal of fortune and that the oppressed and the suffering would be vindicated by

God. There was also a challenge to the wealthy to answer the cry of the poor in action and in deed.

Jon Sobrino, a prominent liberation theologian working in El Salvador, has deeply pondered the existence of the material poor. He believes that the poor have existed, in one form or another, in every age throughout history. For Sobrino and for other theologians around the world, liberation theology represents a response to the poor, to the marginalized, to the non-persons of the world. This includes all whose basic dignities and rights are denied them. Sobrino calls the oppressed, the marginalized, and the exploited the "crucified people," and he maintains that they are the ones whose light shines above all others.

> That people is the historical continuation of the servant of Yahweh, whose humanity is still being disfigured by the sin of the world, whom the powers of this world are still stripping of everything, taking away everything including his life, especially his life.[4]

Coralis and other missioners are motivated to work with the suffering poor by their compassion for the people ravaged by famine, illness, and despair they witness every day. Kenya's current socioeconomic and political situation is fraught with ethical and moral questions such as a lack of freedom, ignorance, disease, ethnic wars, class antagonism, and racial and tribal persecution. No one experiences all these issues more acutely than the women and children. In many parts of Africa a woman's life might have less value than that of a goat or a chicken. (Coralis was surprised to

---

[4] Jon Sobrino, *No Salvation outside the Poor* (Maryknoll, NY: Orbis Books, 2008), 3.

learn that a standard marriage dowry consisted of three
goats!) "I decided that I wanted to work with children because they are used and abused, and women are always the
underdogs," says Coralis.

Beginning Ministry in Mombasa

When she first arrived in Mombasa, nearly fifty years
after Kenya's independence from British colonialism, Coralis discovered a place that was intriguing and mysterious:
"It reminded me of my childhood home in Manila, the
'old town' with Spanish-style buildings and verandas, tropi-
cal fruit and coconut trees, ocean breezes and sultry heat."
Mombasa is the oldest city in Kenya and is composed of a
large community of Africans, Indians (commonly known as
Asians), and Muslims of Arabic origin. Many of the Muslim
women wear the *buibui*, a black garment that covers them
from head to toe with only a sliver left open for their eyes.
Coralis felt immediately at home in Mombasa and knew
it was a good place to begin her ministry. "God's spirit is
very much alive among the Kenyans whom I began to
work with and to serve." In time they would show her
Christ incarnate by working in solidarity as a servant to
empower one another. "I felt humbled by their living faith,
their African spirituality rooted in sharing, a belief of the
interdependency and unity of all creation, in its origin, its
existence and in its final destiny."

One of her first ministries and one that totally absorbed
her for the next ten years was the AIDS Orphans' Project. Initially, it involved getting to know the patients, the
children, their guardians, and their way of life. She visited
many homes along with an experienced social worker who

assessed the patients' conditions and needs. In spite of her struggling Swahili, Coralis tried to establish a relationship with the ailing client and the family. She was amazed that although these families suffered enormous hardships, they were ever hopeful and most appreciative of the visit, often displaying warm smiles. Most families lived in one room, a clay or mud shanty with an earthen floor, thatched roof, and one small window to allow in a slight stream of light. They had no electricity or running water.

One of Coralis's earliest client visits was in the slum of Bangala. It was typical of the hundreds of home visits that would follow over the years: "After traveling from my flat near the 'old town' via *matatu*, a social worker and I walked along a dirt path and over foot bridges made from tree trunks past a ramshackle assortment of mud and cement shanties. Twenty feet below the bridges was broken, jagged earth. We had to walk very carefully on the bridges, balancing ourselves and our packages of food." Coralis eventually made her way to a very small and very dark hut. As her eyes adjusted to the gloomy interior after the brilliant, oppressive noonday sun, she heard someone say, "*Karibuni*," the welcome greeting. "I saw the faces of the couple we were visiting. They were in their early forties but looked much, much older because of their harsh life. The man had AIDS. His legs were covered with huge open sores, and the stench from his infected wounds was overpowering. At first I was repelled by his wounds but then, not knowing why, I quickly was filled with empathy for him. Because he couldn't work, his wife earned a living by buying an illegal brew known as *pombe* that she then transported in a five-liter bucket on top of her head. On her way home, she would often be stopped by a policeman who demanded *chai*, a bribe. If she did not give in to his demand, he would grab the filled bucket and toss it away."

Thirty years ago, the martyred Salvadorian archbishop, Oscar Romero, did not permit himself to be overwhelmed by the dire circumstances he witnessed.

> [W]e cannot do everything, and there is a sense of liberation in realizing that. This enables us to do something, and to do it very well. It may be incomplete, but it is a beginning, a step along the way and an opportunity for the Lord's grace to enter and do the rest.[5]

This was the view Coralis adopted. "I quickly realized that I could not do it all."

The AIDS Pandemic

The AIDS pandemic has cast a long, dark shadow over all of Africa and most acutely Kenya, from its stunning fertile Rift Valley in the west to the beautiful blue-green waters of the Indian Ocean in the east. This panoramic expanse includes some of the most famous national game parks in Africa and is a magnet for foreign tourists. In January 2008 UNAIDS estimated that the number of people living with HIV/AIDS in Kenya was approximately 1.6 to 1.9 million. The number of orphans due to AIDS during this time frame was approximately 1.1 to 1.3 million youths under the age of eighteen.

---

[5] Although the words of this passage are attributed to Oscar Romero, they were never spoken by him. They were, in fact, spoken by John Cardinal Dearden in November 1979 in a homily he gave at a mass for deceased priests (National Catholic Reporter, March 28, 2004).

In the first half of her ministry, Coralis witnessed one death after another from AIDS. When she visited AIDS sufferers, in many instances she surmised that the person she was spending time with would shortly be dead. "But I didn't give up hope; I tried to be present since I knew that each patient was important. They were needed by their children as well as their community." Over the years, while there have been many gains in the battle to stem the disease, there is still no cure. However, since 2004, antiretroviral drugs (ARVs) have become available. Foreign governments began to fund the costs of the drugs, and so the drugs were free for some of Coralis's patients. In 2004, only people with full-blown AIDS were eligible, but around 2005, the ARVs became free for everyone.

These drugs have an impressive record of restoring health and prolonging life despite the side effects they have for some patients. In addition, there has been an increasing availability of testing and counseling services. Nonetheless, the majority of those living with HIV in developing countries remain unaware of their HIV status. Even though emphasis on and access to HIV services for women and children have improved globally, AIDS remains the leading cause of mortality among women of reproductive age. AIDS continues to have a devastating impact on their health, their livelihood, and their overall ability to survive.

Coralis was responsible not only for the orphans, but also for their guardians and others involved in the orphans' lives. The children were all either infected with AIDS or affected by AIDS. The effect of the disease was most profound on the young girls and teenagers. Because of poverty, many sold themselves into prostitution. They either had the disease before becoming sexually active or passed it on after their infection. Even more incredible, sometimes the child's parent or guardian pushed the child into selling herself to help pay the rent or buy food. Winding up as a commercial sex worker, as prostitutes are known in Kenya, is an ever-present fear for the orphans who are girls.

Pretty, feisty, and determined, Zainabu Wanjiru, nineteen years old, is an articulate and confident young Muslim woman. Her mother died of AIDS, and she entered the project in 2002 when she was in Class 2. Zainabu's mother, her maternal aunts, and her other female relatives had all been forced to become commercial sex workers because of extreme poverty. Many of them died of AIDS, leaving numerous orphaned children, including Zainabu, who was raised by her grandmother. "Sometimes I had no food, no breakfast, no lunch, and perhaps something small for supper. I was hungry, but I did not wonder where God was. And even now, grown up, I believe God is there because God has taken me from when I didn't know what would happen to me. I worried that I would get HIV and that I might have to go around sleeping with men just to get money, but that did not happen to me. I said to myself, 'Even though your family has no money, there is no way you are going to sell yourself for money.'" She forcefully articulates her intention not to fall into prostitution. "No, I will not sell myself for a meal!! So I appreciate everything I have, including the little food. I say 'thank you, God.' God came and I am happy with the kind of life I have, and I guess that is what keeps me from selling myself."

What does blessed are the poor mean to Zainabu, a Muslim? "It's like, the poor are blessed because God is always tempting your faith; rich people sometimes do not even remember that God is there. But if you ask someone

(Coralis Salvador)

Nineteen-year-old Zainabu Wanjiru, now a community leader.

who is poor, 'Yes,' he will tell you that God is there because it's like, 'I don't have any money and where will the food come from' and then all of a sudden, you find food. Maybe someone comes and gives you food and you say 'Thank you, God.' It's like God is remembering you in a way so that sometimes you don't realize that it is God who has provided the food. God is there and is providing for every human being." Zainabu graduated from high school in 2009 and is currently undergoing training in community leadership. There is every indication that she will be an effective role model.

The AIDS Orphans

A year into Coralis's mission, primary education was still not free, which made it unattainable for the overwhelming majority of Kenyan children. At that time, the average cost of a primary education was $10 to $15 per child per month. That fee did not include the mandatory uniform, books, or shoes. It is important to remember that most Kenyan families include a number of children. Viewing this lack of education as a great injustice, schooling for the orphaned children quickly became Coralis's primary cause, and it would consume her time during the next nine years.

When Coralis started her ministry in 2001, HIV/AIDS was rampant among Kenya's vast population. People were afraid, and they were also grossly misinformed about the nature of the disease and how it spread. AIDS sufferers were immediately stigmatized by their families and the community. They were seen as contaminated and were to be avoided. Since an AIDS diagnosis was truly a death sentence back then, people were afraid to get tested; they simply did not want to know their status. As the health of many deteriorated, often friends and relatives would not offer to help because it was considered prying; it was impolite to ask about someone else's health.

In July Coralis took over the AIDS Orphans' Project that had been started by Sister Dolores Fortier from the Missionary Sisters of Our Lady of Africa. Sister Dolores, originally from Massachusetts, was one of the first people to recognize that one of the effects of the AIDS pandemic was a rapidly increasing number of orphans and street children. In those early years, generally after the death of one or both parents from AIDS, children had to drop out of school. Usually the remaining parent was also HIV positive, and any other potential guardians had school-age children of their own. In partnership with Community Based Health Care (CBHC), the project was designed to provide orphans with school fees, books, uniforms, and at times, food and medical assistance. When Coralis began running the project, forty-one children were involved. On its tenth anniversary in 2009, she had shepherded more than a thousand orphans, many of whom were infected with the virus themselves. "Reflecting back on the number of children who have blessed my life, I am amazed and grateful. I credit God's hand in these efforts."

One of the project's primary objectives is to offer hope to families affected by HIV/AIDS and especially infected children. "They need to be reassured that God does care and has not abandoned them," says Coralis. The Hebrew Scriptures tell us that it is precisely the poor and forgotten ones, the crucified people, whom God has chosen to bring forth justice to the nations. Thus, the goal of the project is to assure that no child orphaned by HIV/AIDS is deprived of primary education because of a lack of money. From the start, the project has been funded by donations. As administrator, one of Coralis's responsibilities was to look for funding sources. With no formal training in fund-raising, she was not particularly comfortable with this part of the job. It's hard for most of us to ask others for money, even when it's for a good cause. But because of the orphans, Coralis moved beyond her comfort zone in the hope that more orphans could receive an education. She learned to *beg* for her orphans and, in time, developed an impressive list of donors from many countries.

In Kenya, revenge, rage, and despair sometimes motivate AIDS sufferers to purposefully infect as many others as possible and then leave a list of names to be found after their death. Equally disturbing is the prevalent myth in Africa that if a man with AIDS rapes a girl or a baby, he will be cured of AIDS. Coralis witnessed the effects of these practices not only on those victims, but also on the community. In the early years, many communities seemed incapable or unwilling to be involved. Among God's crucified people, where there is great hope, there also exists great, unimaginable evil.

Many dying mothers, as well as a few fathers, made death-bed requests on behalf of their children. Sometimes a mother who was very ill with the end stages of AIDS would take her child in hand and walk great distances to hand the child to Coralis. She always promised a dying mother that the orphans' project would help her children. Many of the orphans remembered years later how their mothers had tried to en-sure their educations before they died.

Joseph Mwanake was one such orphan. He was twelve years old when his dying mother brought him to Coralis to request assistance so he could attend secondary school. Now twenty-two years old, Joseph says, "My mother gave me a gift before she died by bringing me to Coralis and telling me to study. I wondered where God was because life seemed so unfair. I lost both parents, was suffering and struggling because of being born in a poor family. I would get mad at God because I had no one to take care of me like other children." Mwanake became a serious, focused student who kept his mother's dying wishes present in his mind. He applied himself and stayed away from drugs and a myriad of other temptations. Today he is studying at the Nairobi Polytechnic University College to earn a degree in biochemistry. For him, blessed are the poor means that even though his life has seemingly been beset with many challenges, he "keeps remembering God and prays all the time."

Joseph Kabeba was thirteen years old when he joined the project. His bedridden mother knew she was dying of AIDS and wanted to ensure his continued education after her death. Joseph received good grades, and Coralis recognized his potential to continue his education. But he lived with five families, all related, who could barely sustain themselves. Joseph's aunt and guardian wanted him to help support the family and not *waste* time going to school. Coralis was able to locate a sponsor to send him to boarding school, thereby ensuring his education while at the same time getting him out of an unhealthy living situation.

Sadly, Joseph Kabeba fell into drugs, became addicted, and his grades plummeted. In his third year of school, Coralis was on the verge of taking him out of school and giving his place to the next youth on the waiting list. Yet, for some unknown reason, Joseph turned his life around. He exposed the drug situation at school and, with the support of the staff, started to believe in himself again. At twenty-three, it still pains Joseph to recall what he was like on drugs. "I would skip classes and, most hurtful of all, I lied to Mama Coralis." Now he recognizes God's grace and taps into it daily. "There is a just God because God cannot give you more than you can handle. We cannot be like people from the West because they have their way of life and we have our way of life in Kenya. But there is time. Some of us are still learning and some of us are still crying, but we have to feel this way and then we know that God is there."

For Joseph Kabeba, blessed are the poor means "that the rich people don't have anything to lose. The rich have the worldly beauty, and the poor really have to pray to God because each single moment passing is like a miracle: five minutes ago you may feel that you didn't have anything to eat, and ten minutes later you get some twenty shillings (about thirty cents). It is very little but enough to give thanks to God, the one who gives blessings, and that's the meaning of 'blessed are the poor.' The twenty shillings means another minute of life. There is no blessing better from God than one's life." Kabeba believes that "every day of life holds a purpose to fulfill. Each moment that I live is the blessing." Today, he works in business, is a community leader, and is the founder of a support organization for youths addicted to drugs and alcohol.

Jon Sobrino has written that

> The hope of the poor passes through crisis, through epochs of "disenchantment with the immediate," for there do not appear any immediate and calculable outcomes and victories. But there is a faith that overcomes darkness, and there is a hope that triumphs over

disenchantment, as is well shown in poor people's historic patience and their determination to live.[6]

One of the very first orphans involved in the project, Steve Jalango, epitomized this hope. Jalango was a primary-school student when he joined the project after the death of his father. He was motivated to study hard in order to be accepted into the secondary-school program. Devoted to his mother, as he matured he remained focused and determined to make something of himself. Tall and slim with an engaging smile, Steve is articulate, educated, easygoing, and compassionate. He lives in a one-room thatched hut with three siblings. Jalango genuinely believes that God is there for everyone, whether Christian or Muslim. "Poverty is a challenge that God wants us to overcome," he says. He also believes that the challenge of overcoming poverty presents a blessing. "Any good thing from God is a blessing, so for me just being alive is a blessing. God is there for us all. God has come to help, but it is up to the individual to choose to accept the help. When one accepts, then both are blessed. Blessings are not measured in terms of riches or affluence. Blessings are measured in one's relationship with God." Jalango is a seeker of truth who does not blindly accept faith. He is guided by the belief that God's grace envelops him. He sought out Coralis and many others in his pursuit of a deeper meaning for his life. Eventually he became a leader in the youth community and worked closely with the parish priests.

Steve Jalango could easily have chosen to be enticed by free drugs, heroin, cocaine, and marijuana. He could easily have chosen alcohol and the illicit brew made secretly

---

[6] Sobrino, *No Salvation*, 61.

in the slums that is so popular with young men his age. There is also an abundance of drugs coming in through the coastal area of Kenya en route to Europe. Sadly, there is much anecdotal evidence that these drugs are being freely and intentionally distributed to the youth to increase the market for them in Kenya. This developing crisis is known to the government yet is not being addressed. Currently some NGOs (nongovernmental organizations) are leading a movement to shed light on this escalating problem because increasing drug abuse has all the makings of the next pandemic. Rather than turning to this easy path, Jalango tapped into God's gift, and it became his blessing. He is now an outstanding leader in his community, giving back and sharing the fruits of his blessings with others.

Ministry Happens Along the Way

After September 11, 2001, many of Coralis's supporters in the United States wondered how that tragic event would impact her life and ministry. She herself began wondering what she was doing so far away from family and friends. She found herself struggling inwardly. "God's words—'I hold you in the palm of my hand'—helped me stay centered when the pull to return to the U.S. was in my thoughts. I was worried about my adult children's safety and also my sister who worked for one of the affected airlines. Trusting in God saved my sanity." Yet she was living in a predominantly Muslim culture that at the time was being stereotyped as a breeding ground for terrorists. She knew differently, at least in Mombasa, where she encountered Muslims and Christians who were serious about their religious practices. Five times a day the Muslim call to prayer was blasted from huge speakers mounted atop the mosques. Coralis observed that before and after 9/11 Christians, Muslims, Hindus, and those Kenyans practicing indigenous religions lived harmoniously in Mombasa.

In the beginning of her ministry Coralis was fraught with emotion and sadness by the tragedy, the frequent death, and the despair she witnessed. "I credit my mentor, Juliana Karisa, a native Kenyan and a CBHC social worker, for helping me cope with my emotions and get through this difficult time." A very effective and caring social worker, Juliana, a mother of five, is a vibrant, passionate, articulate woman with a deep relationship with God. "I wanted more than anything to be like her. I wanted to master her skills. To me, she was the 'art of social work.'"

Coralis's own transition from a mother of five and a bank administrator to a missionary and social worker evolved over time. Spiritually, she wished for a closer and deeper union with God. "I wanted, selfishly, to inhale the presence of God's abounding love, and I believed it would be more apparent to me if I was serving the marginalized poor."

Theologian Henri Nouwen describes how the transition to ministry works:

> Ministry is not something you do next . . . ministry is the overflow of your love for God and for your fellow human beings. Ministry happens when you participate in the ministry of being with. The whole incarnation, God-with-us, Emmanuel, is first of all being with people. Ministry means that we lift the incarnation—we lift the God who says, "I will be with you." We are precisely where people are vulnerable, not to fix it or change it. That is the unintended fruit of it, but that

is not why you are there. Ministry is being with the
sick, the dying, being with people wherever they are,
whatever their problems. We dare to be with them in
their weakness and trust that if we enter into peoples'
vulnerable places, we will experience immense joy.
That is the mystery of ministry.[7]

In the beginning of her ministry, whenever one of her
clients died, Coralis would turn to Juliana in tears. She in-
vested so much love and care into each client, and when
they died—as so very many of them did—the pain was
unbearable. Kenyans view death very differently from those
of us who live in the West. The word death is unmention-
able; even the obituary pages of the newspapers euphemize
death as a promotion to glory or moving on to heavenly
life. Relatives go to extremes to raise funds to ensure a
traditional burial, which means being buried in one's birth-
place with all the traditional rites observed. Prior to dying,
many of the HIV/AIDS clients are left to fend for themselves. Upon death, however, relatives suddenly appear to
help with the funeral arrangements. This is done to appease
the ancestral spirits and to avoid harm falling on the living
relatives. The AIDS Orphans' Project does not encourage
this practice but instead urges the sick who are near death
to go home and be reconciled with relatives.

In some parts of Kenya when a Kenyan husband dies,
relatives invade the house and take whatever they can, including not only the children, but also every physical item
in the home: makeshift cardboard for a mattress, cooking
pots, rusted used metal containers for stools and chairs!
The mother is also put out of the hut with perhaps only a

---

[7]   Nouwen, *Jesus: A Gospel*, 36.

cardboard box or corrugated metal covering to shelter her under a nearby tree. The relatives then either move into the home or take the children up country. The mother has absolutely no rights, spousal, parental, or otherwise. There are a number of reasons given for this callous traditional practice: for example, the husband's family paid the dowry price, and they want a return on their investment; or there is the assumption that the woman, the wife, brought AIDS into the house.

In time, Coralis became better at coping with constant death. Like Juliana, she became immune to her clients dying; this was in no way cruel but simply a way of carrying on in a difficult profession. Over time she also learned to shed her Western mentality. "At first when I listened to a client's sad story, I felt I had to move quickly to 'fix things,' but after a while I came to realize that sometimes the clients were not very sincere or even honest." Juliana's gift, among many, was her ability to see through made-up stories and outright lies. It was only through a long, slow process that Coralis learned to look at a client's situation and question what was happening beforehand, and speculate on what might happen afterwards if a certain course of action was taken. Juliana and Coralis constantly checked and rechecked with each other when evaluating a problematic situation. Eight years later, after working together day after day, Juliana says laughingly, "Now Coralis is even tougher than I am!" Their mutual respect and regard for each other is palpable and obvious. Coralis adds that she doesn't look for quick fixes anymore; instead she allows a certain amount of time to see what resources may be available. "Sometimes if you help them immediately, it can cause another problem."

This is exactly what happened early in her ministry. Coralis had visited a family in the Miritini slum to evaluate how the family could be helped. There was nothing in the hut except a woman seated on the bare and muddy earthen floor breast-feeding her child. A small and sooty black cooking pot in the corner was surrounded by filthy, worn out plastic cups and plates. The family had not paid the rent in three months. The mother and child had sores and blisters, scabs actually, all over their bodies. A three-year-old son lying on the floor nearby was equally covered with scabs. Quickly, Coralis reasoned that the sores were from sleeping on the bare dried mud. Without telling Juliana, she purchased a piece of new linoleum and brought it to the hut. The mother was so very happy. But when her husband came home, he immediately took it up and

(Maryknoll Mission Archives/Sean Sprague)

Coralis Salvador with Juliana Karisa, a CBHC
social worker who was her mentor.

sold it, using the money to buy illicit brew. A neighbor told the village chief, who in turn confronted the husband. When he refused the chief's demand to do the right thing, the chief beat him with his *urungo*, his symbolic authority stick. The husband then returned the money, buying back the piece of linoleum. When the landlord came to collect the rent and saw the linoleum, he assumed the family had money and was holding back on the rent, so he threw the family out.

Coralis reflects on how she changed in the early years. "I learned to be flexible and adaptable, but most important of all, I learned to be more focused on developing and maintaining good relationships than on immediately trying to fix things. If things didn't work out the way I intended, I accepted it because in the process I developed a relationship."

Patience, never Coralis's strong suit, was seriously challenged many times since the Kenyan tendency is to do things *pole-pole* (slowly). Over time she learned to take things in stride the Kenyan way. People sick with AIDS and in terrible pain would find the strength to smile and show their appreciation because she took the time to visit with them. She began to make a conscious effort to think about the other person first so she could develop a relationship. Then they worked together to find ways to help themselves.

At the beginning of every school year and as the project expanded, Coralis had to turn down some orphans for secondary school. There simply wasn't room, as the project had funding for only so many children. Twins, Alex and Lillian Ochieng, sixteen years old, were a painful example of the lack of space. When their widowed mother died of complications from AIDS, they moved up country to live with their lone, impoverished aunt. On his own volition, Alex made the long trip back to Mombasa to seek assistance from the project so he could continue secondary school. He was earnest, committed, and bright but still, painfully, Coralis had to turn him away. Although she reached out to other institutions for assistance, she was unsuccessful. In spite of this setback, Alex remained prayerful and hopeful. Was this his blessing? When Lillian eventually was married off for a dowry price, Coralis reasoned that that was better than returning to Mombasa and being lured into prostitution.

Coralis summed it up: "I've learned that everything is a gift, the ups and the downs. There can't be light without darkness. You cannot feel joy without sadness. I am called to be 'the salt and the light.' When something bad happens, such as a school girl getting pregnant, I have to help her. It's like dealing with your own children when they are in pain. I go through the same emotions, the trauma, the shock, but in the end, I am just an instrument of the Lord. I realized that it's not for me to solve their problems but rather I'm to be an instrument to help them learn how to solve their own problems. My heart goes out to the people as I try to bring the Lord into any given situation."

Even though Coralis sees tangible fruits of her ministry, she confesses that many times she has "lost her cool." "Some guardians have a way of pressing the right button to ignite my impatience, and if I had my way, I would scream and ask them to get out of my sight! However, in the end, I believe that with the prompting of the Holy Spirit I am able to take a deep breath, seek a quiet moment, and then proceed in a rational way. Of course I get mad! I want to shake the guardians or orphans and say, 'Why are you doing this to yourselves? Why are you resigned to stay where you are in this poverty?' As I myself accept their situations, I realize that perhaps I have planted a seed of discontent or a spark of motivation that may make them want to change their lives. So their situation is a mirror to me, a give and take. I am no longer where I was when I first came. I am a totally different person. I am living on the edge of the kingdom of God and it's a constant struggle to see the kingdom."

Coralis witnessed that many of the poor simply accept their way of life. They are not separated from the Divine. They trust in a higher being and have a certain mentality or belief that accepts the nature of today, even though suffering is involved, but they still hope that things will improve, that things will be different. Their lives are filled with sharing and caring for one another. Such are their blessings.

Chapter 3

Blessed Are Those
Who Are Poor but Truthful

The crucified poor exist all over Africa, especially in the era of the AIDS pandemic. Their anguished faces speak of unmitigated suffering and grief, yet they are oftentimes filled with inexorable hope. It is this hope, true hope, that Coralis witnessed daily in her mission work. And it was the need for compassionate care, the embodiment of social justice, that guided her.

"To be 'in mission' means to share God's love so that we may be one," says Coralis. "We are all called to serve and to love one another and those in need. We, the nonpoor, are called to conversion from a mind-set of self-interest to one of empathy for others. We are challenged to act, simply act, to relieve the suffering of the crucified poor." Love is at the heart of the gospels; love is everything. The simple test of love is this: Do we treat everyone—high and low—as if dealing with Jesus himself, demonstrating his own inclusive and gratuitous love?

Such love is not a dreamy, sentimental, or gushy love, but rather a radical love that calls forth radical action: "For I hungered and you gave me food. I thirsted and you gave me drink, I was an alien and you welcomed me, I was naked and you clothed me, I was ill and you tended me, I was in prison and you came to me. . . . In truth I tell you, whenever you did these things to the lowliest of my brothers, you were doing it to me" (Matthew 25:31–46). In many of the poor, hope is vibrantly alive because they witness God's arms enfolding them through the missioners who risk walking with them.

Luke's Beatitudes in the New Testament

Jesus' partiality for the poor is in complete harmony with the prophets of the Hebrew Scriptures and in particular with Isaiah. Indeed, it is precisely the poor and forgotten ones whom God has chosen to "bring forth justice to the nations" (Isaiah 42:1). Leonardo Boff, a liberation theologian, explains that

> the poor are the chosen ones of God and his Messiah, not because they are ready and adorned with moral virtues, but because they are poor. The reason is not in the poor ones, but in God, who wants to choose them. This is the meaning of the blessedness of the poor, according to St. Luke, the concrete and historical poor, made poor and objects of exploitation, who will be the first beneficiaries of the goods of the Kingdom, which are supported in justice, without which no good has a firm base.[1]

But what does this mean? Like other missioners working among the poor in Africa, Latin America, and Asia, Coralis witnessed people living in horrible conditions, working hard to scratch out a living. Yet many of these people do not see themselves as poor. It should be noted, though, that she also witnessed other marginalized poor whose status

---

[1] Leonardo Boff, *The Maternal Face of God: The Feminine and Its Religious Expressions* (New York: Harper & Row, 1987), 55.

was simply overwhelming and left them without hope, unable to move in any direction toward hope. Those who do not envision themselves as poor simply see their lives and status in a given snapshot of time, without judgment or rancor. If great sadness occurs, they believe that this too will pass. Many of the marginalized poor have a different way of perceiving their circumstances. They continue to have hope and joy, where we Westerners, given a similar scenario, would probably simply give up. Is this simply a means of survival? Or is this their blessing?

Lucy, a young mother of two, has AIDS. Her five-year-old daughter is HIV positive. The family lives in the village of Chaani in a mud hut with a dirt floor and a thatched roof that leaks during the rainy season. The family has one bed with an old mattress that rests on the floor. Kenyan standards would deem their living arrangements to be considered pretty good. Many of the AIDS orphans don't even have a bed. Lucy's family sleeps on a piece of plastic to keep the insects from biting them. Every time Coralis visits she is amazed at how neat Lucy's home is. White lace covers the stools, chairs, and table, and Lucy always greets Coralis with a warm, beautiful smile. She is proud of her small home, and she doesn't see herself as poor. Coralis delivers flour, salt, oil, and sugar. Lucy washes clothes to earn money; however, every time a new infection invades her body, she is unable to work. This is the reality of AIDS. Even so, sometimes Lucy will decline the offered food, saying "I still have salt or sugar from last week, give it to someone else!" Coralis was astonished at her generosity and honesty. "Lucy was always confident that God would provide the food for her family when she was in need." Lucy died in 2003 and her two daughters were taken up country by their uncle.

Not everyone is like Lucy. Sometimes mothers think they have no option but to prostitute themselves, and sometimes even their children, simply to be able to buy some food or to pay the rent. Sometimes an AIDS sufferer sells a life-saving medication for a meager food ration in order to stay alive. And there are some HIV-negative mothers who are so desperate to educate their children that they actually contract AIDS on purpose in order to receive the benefits. "Are you crazy? Your good health is your blessing!!" Coralis would say to these women. "You don't have to do this. There are other options." Stories like these challenge our understanding of Christ's assurances of blessings to the poor.

Many of Coralis's orphans live in Bangala, the largest slum in Mombasa. Here she met Father Gabe Dolan, a Kiltegan priest from Ireland who has served in Kenya since 1982. He is vocal, liberal, and a serious irritant to both the

(Coralis Salvador)

Coralis's home visit with Lucy and one of her daughters.

government and the hierarchy of the Catholic Church. A tall man with an easy smile and a commanding and reassuring manner, Father Dolan is in constant motion. He writes a weekly column for a Kenyan national newspaper, *The Daily Nation*, in which he takes on the power structure and corruption of the Christian and Islamic institutions in Kenya as well as the government. Coralis constantly worries about his safety; in Kenya it's not unusual for people to simply disappear or wind up dead, or if foreign, to be expelled from the country.

"The poor whom I serve have great dignity, they want to improve," says Father Dolan. "They have very high aspirations and goals; their children are central, and they want them educated. In Luke's beatitudes, Jesus refers to the dignified poor. In the urban slums of Kenya, people try every means possible to feed their children and work on their behalf. For them, poverty is an evil that must be fought against on a daily basis. There is a difference, however, between poverty and the poor. We all must fight poverty as an institution, as we would a disease. Being poor, on the other hand, is just a condition that can be changed. The poor have great human wisdom and human values. They must shape their own destiny, and there is great dignity in this. Their greatest motivation is that their children receive an education, and the rich should be called upon to help fulfill this goal."

Father Dolan adds, "For the materially poor, it would seem that there is nothing 'blessed' about being destitute. However, even being destitute, they have hope that they can still turn things around. Christ means 'blessed' are those who are working every day and getting by even though they are struggling. There is still great dignity in those who struggle to get by even in the poorest of settings. They must, however, be in on the planning of their destiny, or they will simply be beneficiaries, which leads to dependency." Indeed, one of the essential goals of the AIDS Orphans' Project is to foster eventual independence of the orphans and their guardians. Coralis explains, "We don't foster dependence. It is our goal to get people up on their feet and functioning as a family unit themselves. The project supports the education of the orphans so that they can become contributing members of the community and lighten the burdens on the struggling family."

Father Dolan has tried to be salt and light. His ministry brings the light of liberation, although he does not know exactly what will happen next. "The light is solidarity with the poor. We are not gatekeepers, but distributors of the light and I don't know exactly who will be affected by the light." For him, the blessings of bringing light to the poor are best exemplified when he calls for leaders to tackle a problem in the community and people step forward and demonstrate outstanding leadership. He finds this absolutely remarkable: "They have come to serve their community even though they do not have any money." It is that sense of empowerment that the AIDS Orphans' Project fosters in each of its students in the hope of moving the next generation toward autonomy. This is already the status of orphans Steve Jalango, Joseph Kabeba, and Zainabu Wanjiru, who have all moved beyond the status of orphans and into the status of community leaders.

Coralis agrees wholeheartedly with Dolan. To her, one of the main attributes of a missioner is to be the salt and the light. A number of community health volunteers are HIV positive themselves. She explains, "They bring care and love for their neighbors as they live out their faith. They are truly the 'salt and light' of their own community and it brings joy to me to witness their strength." Jon Sobrino describes how this happens: "Like the lamp in the gospel, they illuminate their surroundings. They can then become the salt that gives flavor and the leaven that makes the dough expand, which means that they produce salvation beyond themselves."[2]

When asked where Christ is in the slums of Mombasa, Dolan responds, "Christ is there, and it's only for us to see him, and you see that when you relate to the people. We must be mindful that it is for us to reach out and to see God. God is in every one of these people who find hope in his message." Where is the demonstrative evidence of God's presence in the lives of these unfortunate men, women, and children? Joseph Nangle, a long-time Franciscan missionary and activist, argues that "each of us, and all who follow Jesus, have to be the evidence of that loving, caring God—or else no such evidence exists."[3]

Workshops of Empowerment

The AIDS Orphans' Project was originally established to pay for primary-school fees, books, and uniforms, but over the years Coralis took it in a more holistic direction. She realized the need to initiate workshops for the orphans and their guardians so they could really get to know each other. She also used the workshops as a vehicle for healing and to

---

[2] Jon Sobrino, *No Salvation Outside the Poor* (Maryknoll, NY: Orbis Books, 2008), 63.

[3] Joseph Nangle et al., *St. Francis and the Foolishness of God* (Maryknoll, NY: Orbis Books, 2004), 104.

let the orphans know they were not the only ones suffering. Coralis peppered the kids with questions to get them thinking: "What are your dreams? What are your hopes? What are you feeling about your reality? Are you hurting, angry, frustrated?" Coralis quickly realized that the orphans had never been asked these provocative questions. It was simply not a part of their culture. Their answers were an eye-opener for her. The orphans longed for their deceased parents, and they craved the barest basic necessities of life that we in the West take for granted. They dreamed of becoming pilots, doctors, lawyers, teachers—and yes, some of the kids just wanted a pair of shoes! Coralis told them time and again that they were special, that they were children of God, and that they could aspire to be anything they wanted to be.

These workshops generally took place each year during the school breaks in April, August, and December. In addition to the obvious goal of empowerment, they were also a simple way to keep the kids off the street. It was far too easy for these youths to be lured into sex, petty crime, and the ever-increasing availability of drugs. Many of the workshops also included sports, drama, and song and dance competitions. The opportunity to develop self-esteem and team-building was a bonus. "I would smile inwardly to myself when I saw a child beginning to take on a leadership role among the nucleus of orphans," Coralis says with satisfaction.

Elizabeth Mugo, sixty years old, a doting wife, mother of eight, and grandmother to four, is an integral component of the workshops. Known as Mrs. Mugo by the orphans, this short, stocky woman, buoyant with energy, exhibits a kind, caring, self-sacrificing presence. Over time she trained the

health-care workers and took courses to facilitate workshops for both children and adults on AIDS awareness, the
development of self-esteem, and techniques for empowerment. Mrs. Mugo collaborated with Coralis time and again
regarding the planning and execution of each of the workshops. They included Adventures Unlimited workshops for
primary-age children and Education for Life workshops for
children in Class 8 through high school as well as day-long
retreats for spiritual reflection. Eventually Coralis turned
over many of these programs to Kenyans—a missioner cannot stay forever!

Coralis often teamed up with Emmah Ndonye, a field
worker with the Justice and Peace Office of the Archdio-
cese of Mombasa. Emmah, a tenacious Kenyan, has a sharp
intellect and an indomitable spirit to tell it like it is. She is
tough, strident, and incredibly critical of what she perceives
as the failures of the Kenyan society. She is physically im-
posing and rarely considers how the very act of challenging
authority may impact her own professional growth. Her
job is to travel the vast geographical area known as Mombasa West to meet with tribal chiefs, volunteer community
leaders called animators, and with the health-care workers
and the villagers. Extremely articulate, Emmah educates, she
prods, and she chastises and challenges the antiquated and
inequitable tribal customs and governmental and societal
injustices on behalf of all the people she serves.

One such unjust tribal custom is female genital mutila-
tion, or female circumcision. Even though outlawed, certain
tribes still practice this custom. The Justice and Peace workers undertake training for the community about children's
rights, and they also offer a more appropriate alternative
solution for a coming of age or rite of passage ceremony. An-

other traditional practice she opposes is the practice of early marriages. Girls as young as five can be betrothed to much older men, and when such a girl reaches her menstrual age, she is moved into the man's home, sometimes as a second or third wife. These very young wives will often become pregnant and give birth before their bodies are ready for it. Another major problem is that far too often boys and girls are kept out of school to work as laborers or to become street children begging for money for the family.

When Mrs. Mugo and Emmah taught the youths about human rights, the risks involved in drugs and alcohol, their social responsibilities, or simply socialized with them, the focus was always on letting them know they were not alone and that their lives had great value as they were children of God.

The Grandmothers and Guardians

As the number of orphans in Kenya increased dramatically because of late detection, no testing, stigmatization, or fear, the burden of raising the orphaned children was usually thrust upon the grandparents. Sadly, it is estimated that approximately 75 percent of the guardians are HIV positive themselves. When there are no surviving grandparents, the selection of guardians is both arbitrary and haphazard. There are no legalities or formalities, and finding guardians for the orphans is frequently a difficult task. Who is willing to step up and take the orphan(s)? Most of the time, it is a relative who agrees to assume the role.

Coralis often worked with Felisita, a grandmother and guardian to seven grandchildren, ages ten to nineteen, six girls and one boy. Felisita's three daughters had all died of AIDS. A tall, lean woman, Felisita's face is etched with withering lines, betraying her hard life. After raising one family, now she must do it all over again. Nonetheless, she is filled with love for her grandchildren.

Felisita earns a living selling hot lunch meals at her small outdoor food stand. The family lives in one rented room within a larger cement structure. Such structures do not qualify as slums because they are permanent. They generally consist of eight separate eight-by-ten-foot rooms, each housing a different family of up to ten members. The rooms are divided by a common hallway that is used as a temporary common kitchen, and the hallway is lined with *jikos*, small charcoal stoves that are smoky with soot. The latrines are outside in a common courtyard. Felisita is always in front of the *jiko*, preparing dishes to sell. Although Felisita speaks only Luo, her tribal language, she manages to communicate through her grandchildren who speak Sheng (a colloquial combination of Swahili and English).

For Felisita, love means dying to oneself, showing utter selflessness in serving family and others. Now in her late fifties, Felisita should be enjoying old age, but instead she is raising another generation of children, and fortunately the AIDS Project helps pay her grandchildren's tuition. In the future, the elder children will be expected to contribute to the financial support and care of the younger children. Coralis reports that "Felisita has tapped into the Lord's grace and given it selflessly to her grandchildren. She doesn't complain, nor is she bitter. Instead, her heart exudes warmth and joy!"

In 2003, before antiretroviral drugs (ARVs) were available without charge, the number of AIDS orphans was increasing, as was the need for guardians. However, even after

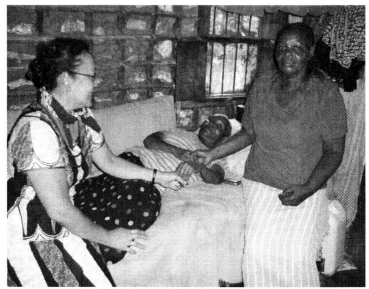

(Coralis Salvador)

Coralis and Adrian Kamau visiting with Mary Wanjiku,
a grandmother caring for five orphaned grandchildren.

the availability of ARVs, the number of orphans continued
to increase. As a result, one of the project's primary goals
was to help train and empower the new guardians. Approximately fifty to sixty guardians participated in a program to
teach them about microfinancing. Sadly, Coralis's attempts
to introduce the concept of microfinancing and lending
failed. By 2010, Coralis deemed this the single most significant disappointment in her ministry. She concluded that
there were many reasons why the program failed. To begin
with, the vast majority of guardians couldn't read or write,
and many didn't have a steady income. Many were also
HIV positive, and their debilitating health issues made them
unreliable participants. Also, some of the guardians simply

did not want to work. Microfinancing is targeted to the active poor or the poor with a purpose. By no means is it a program of handouts. In addition, a number of guardians simply did not want to work that much harder to support the additional children. Yet generating income was never the ultimate goal. Coralis recalls, "The overwhelming goal was to give the guardians a sense of 'wholeness,' the feeling that they were capable of doing something important. They needed to feel empowered in spite of their own sickness. I did not want them to simply wait for death, but rather to be an active part of life."

While many guardians are well meaning, the additional burden of another child is often too great because they are already stretched to the limit. This is especially true in households where family members have AIDS and are required to take ARVs. A major impediment to the success of the medication is the lack of sustainable nutrition. Despite the ready availability of free drugs, many people continue to die because of starvation. Another significant challenge is that some infected with AIDS have turned the ARVs into a business. Many working-class people keep their status secret out of fear of losing their jobs. They buy their drugs from the poor who have given up taking the drugs either because they did not comply with the needed regimen or the drug's side effects were too devastating when taken on an empty stomach.

And sadly there are also instances when the guardian family treats the orphan like hired help but without any pay. These orphans are so overworked that they have no time for school. Frequently Coralis would visit these families and plead with them to allow a child time to study. Sometimes this worked, and sometimes it didn't.

About halfway through her ministry, Chizi, a big-hearted grandmother guardian, came into Coralis's life. Chizi, a marginalized widow and invisible to many, lived in Bomu, a village west of Mombasa. Five of her seven children had died of AIDS, leaving her to care for eight grandchildren from three to thirteen, two of whom are HIV positive. Chizi's attitude of care, hope, and trust in the Lord challenged Coralis's own spiritual journey. She lovingly recalls, "Chizi made Christ very much alive in everything she did because of her sacrifices on behalf of her grandchildren. She made me wonder if I was fully living my call to 'go in peace to serve the Lord.' I came to mission to experience union with the Lord, and I was undergoing that union with Felisita, Chizi, and my other guardians, and, of course, the orphans!"

In the very rare instances when no guardians, relatives, or foster family can be identified, the only alternative is to place the child in an orphanage. It's anathema in the Kenyan culture for a child to be placed in this setting. It is the absolute last recourse. In her ten years of ministry with the orphans, Coralis was brokenhearted when she had no alternative for two children other than placing them in an orphanage.

In mid 2002, Salama, thirty-eight years old and an HIV-positive mother, died. She had been a patient of the Community Based Health Care (CBHC) program, and she left five children, ages four to nineteen. Three of the children, two boys and one girl, were supported by the Orphans' Project. The eldest child, Darius, nineteen years old, informed Coralis that he would be responsible for his four younger siblings since he had a job as a *tout* (conductor) on the Mikindani-Mombasa *matatu* route. The two youngest were Naomi and Sara, nine and four years old. Sara was HIV positive. The two boys, Samson and Crispin, fourteen and sixteen, decided to quit school. Juliana told Coralis that it was not "safe" for the two young girls to be left alone with the brothers. "We were concerned about the physical safety of the girls who lived in the slums of Mikindani. At a certain time of day, it is simply not safe for girls to walk home alone as roving drunken men and boys might prey on them, knowing that there was no parent to care for them." As a result, CBHC health workers and Juliana followed up and made regular visits to the family.

In 2002 on Christmas Day, as part of her usual holiday routine, Coralis brought food and treats to the family. On her way there, she was horrified to find Naomi and Sara wandering aimlessly in the slum. Coralis led them back to their mud hut, but the brothers were nowhere to be found. Having decided to take the girls out for a Christmas treat, she left the food and informed a neighbor. They went to visit Rachael, a member of a well-off Kenyan family who invited them for tea. The girls were very excited, especially because they had never been in a car before.

As Coralis and Rachel chatted over tea on the outside veranda, the girls were too excited to eat. They wanted to explore. As Naomi made her way into the house to look around at so many unfamiliar objects—picture frames, crystal, ashtrays, candles—she was mesmerized, and Coralis was anxious that she might break something. Sara went toward the beautiful garden to explore.

As Coralis and Rachel were sitting talking, Coralis noticed that Sara was ripping leaves off a shrub in handfuls as large as her tiny fingers could hold. She quickly selected the best leaves, put them in her mouth, and chewed. Thinking that the child was just playing with the leaves, Coralis told Naomi to tell Sara to stop. "Oh," Naomi told Coralis, as casual as ever, "Sara thinks it's *bhangi* (a hemp plant commonly used as a drug). Shocked that these young girls had been exposed to *bhangi*, "I asked Naomi how they knew about this plant. She said her brothers bring it home and all of the kids chew it. Sometimes it quells their pangs of hunger. I was boiling angry inside at the neglect of these girls, and knew immediately that they could not stay with their brothers. I brought them home and waited for their brothers to return. Since it was getting dark and I did not feel safe, I told the neighbor to tell the brothers that I wanted to talk to them. Then I immediately called Juliana and told her we had to get the kids out of there."

The following week, Juliana and Coralis arranged to meet with nineteen-year-old Darius in the office. However, before the meeting could take place, the village chief told Coralis that Darius had been arrested and taken to the police station for beating up Naomi. That night Darius had come home high on *bhangi* and was angry that Naomi had not prepared the *ugali*, their staple food of corn flour. When he beat her up, a neighbor reported the incident to the chief. In the end Darius was only given a warning.

Coralis and Juliana met with a remorseful Darius, as they needed his permission to remove the girls from his guardianship. Darius told them that he could no longer care for the two girls and that they had no relatives who could take them. Coralis recalls, "We originally placed the sisters together in an orphanage for HIV-positive kids in Kilifi, to the north of Mombasa. After three months, Naomi ran away and made it back to her home in the slums. She had traveled eighty kilometers by herself. Darius called me to say that she was with him. As a runaway, Naomi was not allowed back in the orphanage." Eventually Coralis was able to place Naomi in a home for street girls in Kiembeni: "Juliana and I would visit the girls. Naomi is now in secondary school, doing well academically and is the star goalkeeper for the girls' soccer team. Sara is in Class 6, taking the ARVs, and is healthy. The brothers regularly visit their sisters and bring Naomi home for special occasions. In the end, I couldn't fault Darius. He has his weaknesses, but he did the right thing in letting us place his sisters outside the home."

Free Primary Education Is Not Really Free

In the beginning of 2003 Kenyans felt triumphant as a result of a national election when the current president was constitutionally barred from reelection and retired. This turn of events ushered in a new beginning, a new life, a new positive spirit, an air of *unbwoggable*, meaning unshaken determination to succeed. Coralis was excited to witness what everyone hoped would be the beginning of a magnificent transition. After twenty-four years of one-man rule, change was happening. People were euphoric and danced in the streets. Coralis told her donors, "If things go well for the Kenyans, perhaps our work here will end, and it will be time to move on to where there are greater needs." However, the prophecy of renewal would not come to pass.

One factor that did change for the better was that primary education became free and compulsory for all children. The AIDS Orphans' Project, which originally assisted only with primary education, was able to expand, and the numbers of orphans it assisted and services it provided were expanded to include secondary-school sponsorship. Even though tuition was free, however, it did not cover the expenses for uniforms and other school materials. In Kenya, if a child does not have the fees to purchase these items, they are prohibited from attending school, whether or not the requirement to attend school is compulsory. This placed enormous burdens on the poor.

Free education gave rise to difficult interactions with some mothers and guardians. For example, Grace, an on-and-off able-bodied mother, demanded that she receive the money that would have gone to her daughter's education before the government started paying for it. Grace would not be mollified and screamed, "That money belongs to my child!" as if her child had actually earned it. For weeks, Grace continued to beg, taunt, and implore Coralis, demanding that the money for future tuition belonged to her. Shouting matches ensued. "Don't you understand that now that the money is not going to your child's tuition, we can use it to buy more uniforms for children not yet in the program," Coralis explained. Time and again, Coralis lost her pleasant demeanor and exploded: "This money is not going into anyone's pocket! It's for the other children's needs!" Coralis simply could not make Grace understand that whatever funds became available as a result of the free education went to support another orphan. The disagreement finally ended in a stalemate, and Coralis asked a colleague to deal with Grace. Coralis's anger and frustration about the "Grace incident," and her entitlement mentality, is palpable even years later.

Grace's attitude was hardly unique. Kenya and other developing countries have an entire class of people that face the challenge of poverty, not through sweat and hard work, but by begging and a sense of entitlement. Coralis continues to wonder if "the Graces" of this world have opened up to their blessings. "Christ will not force his blessing, we have to choose it, and we are clearly expected to work toward it," she believes. Like Coralis, Kenyans, such as Emmah, have no patience for the poor who have made poverty a job. Emmah noted, "People are trying to use poverty as a tool, as an advantage. I am seeing a lot of ignorance in the people in the sense that 'my poverty is a status for me to gain' instead of seeing 'my poverty as a challenge for me to work through or to move ahead.' The issue is that the blessing is not a question of using poverty as a tool to gain. No! The blessing will be 'I see my poverty as a challenge for me to make a move forward; to give me determination and also to give me inspiration and hope.'" This sense of opportunism on the part of the materially poor was articulated not only by Emmah, but also by Juliana, Coralis's mentor, who believes that "Christ's 'blessing' carries with it the obligation to be 'poor and truthful.'" Incredibly, not only did professionals such as Juliana articulate the requirements of honesty, integrity, and hard work, so did some of the orphans themselves.

By the time he was fifteen years old, Collins Onyango had lost both of his parents as well as his sister to AIDS. Collins is a very handsome and caring young man, as Coralis says, "both inside and outside." His ability to articulate difficult theological concepts is impressive. Collins believes that "Poverty is a challenge in life but through hard work and faith in God, you can grow out of poverty. Sometimes through the challenges of poverty, some people resort to devil worshiping. But, devil worship is not a solution to poverty, but instead, it creates more challenges in life."

Over the years Coralis has encountered devil worship, a cult-like phenomenon, among the orphans. Devil worship is not uncommon among the Kenyan people. Witchcraft, the use of supernatural or magical powers, is also commonplace. Fred, an "A" student, had a dramatic drop in his grades during the third term of Form 2, and he attributed his poor academic performance to witchcraft. He concluded that his notes and books had been stolen by his fellow classmates and given to a witch doctor in order to ruin his academic standing. Coralis consulted with the project's social worker and confirmed that a large percentage of the population in the village of Miritini believe in witchcraft and utilize a witch doctor to do harm to persons they consider a threat. Apparently some students were envious of Fred's performance. In the end, the project referred Fred to a priest who was trained to deal with such situations, and after some counseling his grades did improve. Fred eventually became an active member of his evangelical church.

The concept of fairness with regard to poverty in developing nations in the Global South generally winds up involving some form of theological discussions. Is it fair that God allows these things to happen? The "why me, God?" question has endured since the time of Job in the Hebrew Scriptures. Collins reflected in this way: "There was a moment in life when I sat down and thought of these things years after my father passed away because I was too young to think about it when my father actually died. I was missing a father's love and then I knew that there was something I was lacking. I saw other families around me, and I began to ask God why this was happening to me. I saw other parents living, and yet I could not see my parents. When I was in Form 2 and my mother passed away I kept on crying, and then I sat down and thought about the situation and determined that this is the plan of life. This is God's plan that someone will live for a certain number of years, and God looks at how that person lived when alive. For me, through the death of my parents, especially through the death of my mother, I got into the AIDS Orphans' Project. 'Blessed are the poor' means 'poor and hardworking' and 'poor and determined' because you cannot get blessings when you don't have determination. You have to be determined and you also have to believe that this thing will happen to me and you have to work hard for it. 'Blessed are the poor' means that if you have determination to better yourself, that is the blessing because you have to be determined to do something. The phrase is about your heart. So it's a decision that someone has to make on his own. God is there for everybody, and if you know that you feel God is there for you, then God is on his way but has not reached you yet. Then the only thing for you to do is to make a choice to welcome God in your life, and God will be there for you."

When asked "How is God there for the street boys begging and on drugs or the girls trafficked into prostitution?" Collins replies, "God is there for them because every day they breathe, they walk, they see the day. Maybe there is no one to care for the street boys but God is there because they can breathe, they walk, then you are OK." Collins was asked another question: "Theologically, what is so blessed about no food, no school, and AIDS?" He replied, "For you to understand this you have to go inside your heart to get the true and deep meaning. God himself cannot come from heaven and bring food or clothing to the poor, but this means that God uses the rich who will offer help to the poor. This is how I see the AIDS Orphans' Project; the rich ones from the United States and the United Kingdom are coming to help the poor of Kenya."

Reflecting on her own developing spirituality in mission, Coralis was acutely aware that her approach and outlook on life were evolving and becoming more open, and she was able to be more present in the moment. As her lifestyle was slowly becoming integrated and intertwined with the reality of others, she reflected on Jesus' promise that the "poor will always be with you" (John 12:8). Believing that she was being blessed through the poor, she was finding a new self and a deeper relationship with God.

Chapter 4

Blessed Are Those
Who Are Poor but Have Spirit

Drought and Famine

The year of 2005 in Kenya was a year of unprecedented drought. Many Kenyans were starving along with their cattle and poultry. In Mombasa, a large portion of the population, including the clients of Coralis, had no food. Even though "starving" was to some degree a way of life, the drought intensified the people's suffering. Even purchasing a bag of corn flour, a basic staple, was unaffordable due to dramatic price increases. In some of the shanty towns, the number of emaciated children and the elderly was unprecedented, a cruel fact of nature. Those rural areas from Mivumoni in the south to Kitale in the west were unaffected by the drought, and subsistence farmers in these areas were sensitive to the suffering of their sisters and brothers. They donated crops such as corn, cassava, beans, and fruit from their own meager *shamba* or small farms. With no fanfare, piles of food started to appear on the steps of mosques and churches as the miracle of the loaves and fishes played out again and again. The lay missioners also trimmed down their expenses, using their extra money to buy additional flour and beans.

Solidarity with people who have no food became the theme of the 2006 Lenten season. This period of forty days of the liturgical calendar of Christian churches is a season of prayer, penance, and acts of charity. Mombasa's archbishop, Boniface Lele, had grown up in rural Kenya and witnessed many droughts. A highly spiritual and contemplative man, he shows great sensitivity to the needs of the people and does not resort to mere platitudes. Stoutly built, with a constant smile, he shuns the institutional trappings of his office. Appearing in public without a collar and driving his own car, he demonstrates his great sense of humor and is always very approachable. He has a natural and uncanny way of making people feel relaxed and his equal. Coralis and the bishop often share a meditational rite known as centering prayer, a method of silent prayer that prepares a person to receive the gift of God's presence through contemplation. Praying together silently, they developed a strong bond.

"We believe that Jesus gave a new meaning to human suffering; that God accompanies the one who suffers especially if that one who suffers believes that God is with him or her and that it [the suffering] is not punishment," says Lele. "This is a special gift that we receive through Jesus Christ and his passion, which was so painful, so lonesome. We remember Jesus saying, 'Father, why have you forsaken me?' but then he also said, 'Into your hands, Lord, I commend my spirit.' In suffering we have a tendency to feel that we are alone, that we are rejected. As a man Jesus experienced this, but because Jesus trusted in God he had the courage to feel pain. Accompaniment by God does not lessen the pain but gives it meaning; we are in solidarity with God and, with the resurrection, have hope for final liberation." The archbishop's words affirmed for Coralis what she already knew, that God is with the people in their suffering. Coralis says, "It is so Kenyan! They see things so differently. They view suffering as a part of life that someday will pass. Their hope never diminishes; this is their blessing."

Life in Kenya can be very hard: drought, insufficient food, water drawn from dirty ponds, little or no education, the AIDS pandemic, the rape of young girls and women, death, forests stripped bare to provide fuel for cooking, drug cartels, corrupt government at all levels, inadequate police protection, bribes. The list goes on and on. Given this list, my question surfaces again: What's so blessed about being poor?

During the drought Archbishop Lele asked everyone, regardless of religious practices, to come to the aid of their sisters and brothers in dire need. He asked the Kenyan people not to wait for outsiders to bring aid but to work together to solve their own problems and to share with one another. As a result, various communities, including students from private schools, shared food from their pantries. Muslims, Christians, non-Christians, and businesspeople came forward with sacks of flour, rice, beans, and more. For Coralis this was a beautiful act of the Lord providing for the poor through each person who came forward in love.

Mothers Coping with Violent Tragedy

Of all the hundreds of orphans Coralis got to know over the years, in addition to Esha, the stories of Jonathan and another orphan named Lulu simply broke her heart. Jonathan had been involved in project activities for about three years. He and his HIV-positive mother lived in the slum of Kibarani. Jonathan was a typical fourteen-year-old Kenyan boy, lean and outgoing, and not very serious about school. He preferred spending time with his friends. Right after finishing primary school, Jonathan was beaten to death in broad daylight by his friends when he refused to give up a bracelet he wore, a fake trinket with no appreciable value. When his mother told Coralis what had happened, she spoke in a soft, composed, collected manner. She had no anger or other emotion, just the simple recognition that her son was now dead. Coralis gasped, she was shocked not only by Jonathan's senseless death, but by his mother's calm reaction. As she and the mother embraced and Coralis sobbed on her shoulder, the mother remained composed and tried to comfort Coralis. Where was Jonathan's mother's rage, her anguish? Coralis slowly realized that this mother's demeanor didn't indicate that she didn't love her son; instead it was a simple recognition that they live in a place where violence is an everyday part of life. She is not alone, as many Kenyans seem resigned to violence as a part of living.

Coralis met five-year-old Lulu, in November 2006 in Chaani during one of her home visits with Juliana. They were visiting Edwina, a new HIV-positive client, to determine whether her two children were eligible for the AIDS Orphans' Project. Coralis was seated on a chair in the small room and a little girl, Lulu, dressed in a faded blue jumper with no shoes, was seated quietly next to her. Coralis casually asked, "Who is this child?" She was told that the child was Edwina's great niece who "had just been raped." As Coralis and Juliana both questioned the aunt about the circumstances of the attack, Coralis reached for Lulu, hugged her and placed her on her lap to comfort her. Lulu allowed herself to be cradled in Coralis's arms.

Coralis was in a rage. The rapes seemed never ending. In addition to Lulu, a father had recently raped his two daughters ages eight and eleven, and a nine-month-old in-

Coralis with a child victim of rape.

fant had been sexually abused by someone known to the family. Even though Coralis reported these crimes to the Children's Office, the Justice and Peace workers, and the police, the rapes continued. The Children's Office is a governmental entity charged with the responsibility of protecting children's rights. It has one office in the center of Mombasa. Unable to handle the volume of cases, it has trained volunteers from each community to conduct field investigations and reports. Either they are overwhelmed, or such crimes fall on deaf ears. Even if there is an appropriate investigation, the rape of women and children is not regarded as a serious crime by the judicial system. Emmah, from the Justice and Peace Office, did gather the community together to encourage and help protect their children, but the rapes still continue.

During this time, Coralis also heard of multiple rapes of children along the southern border of Kenya with Tanzania. The Justice and Peace workers decided to go to Taveta, southwest of Mombasa at the foot of Mount Kilmanjaro, to investigate. This was during Susan's first trip in 2006 when she was a short-term volunteer in Mombasa working on human rights for the Justice and Peace Office. Susan accompanied Emmah as part of the team so she could report back to Coralis.

The five-hour drive to Taveta is extremely arduous even in a four-wheel-drive vehicle as the dirt roads are pockmarked with deep ruts. The ride is agonizingly bumpy, yet it goes through Tsavo West, one of the largest and most magnificent national parks. The vast, natural beauty is breathtaking with baobab trees with trunks akin to elephant legs, sturdy, thick, and gray with no foliage. The earth is red clay with multiple ant hills erupting from the plains, some as tall as the Kenyans themselves. Herds of elephants, zebras, gazelles, waterbucks, and giraffes grazed nearby, and now and then traversed the road. The natural beauty was so exciting and stunning that the purpose of the visit and the horror of the investigation were forgotten. Upon arriving in Taveta, the awesome expanse of magnificent Mount Kilimanjaro came into view.

The group was scheduled to stay overnight in Taveta, so they would have enough time to adequately complete the necessary fact-finding. They met with the parish priest and community leaders, who described the case of a two-year-old girl who had been raped the previous week. The child, brutally beaten, was hospitalized and not allowed to leave because her family didn't have the $20 needed to pay the hospital charges. As the group was trying to absorb this inequity, the community lamented about not being able to stop these rapes. What amazed the group of investigators was that there was no screaming, no yelling, no pounding of fists, or calling for retribution. The parents seemed simply resigned to the rape of children as a circumstance of their existence.

Susan and Annie, a retired law-enforcement officer from the United States, suggested that the residents start "Community Watch" groups in which neighbors watch out for neighbors, but the people didn't seem to understand. They *knew* who the rapist was, but they couldn't persuade the authorities to take any action. They said that the authorities are of a mind-set that a rape case takes a lot of work, so rape is far down on their list of priorities, and it appears that the rapists continue with impunity.

That trip and meeting with the community had a profound impact on Susan. Of course they gave the priest the $20 to have the child discharged from the hospital, but the very practice of holding victims hostage, knowing full well that the family could not pay the release price, seemed beyond barbaric. The investigators also learned of a local custom, based on witchcraft, that was equally repugnant. Once a woman becomes pregnant, she stays in a shanty for six months. She has no intercourse with her husband and instead gives permission for him to have sex with their daughter(s). To this day, the Taveta experience haunts Susan.

Fortunately, there have been changes since that initial visit. Through the efforts of the Peace and Justice Program, a field officer now follows up on all reported cases of rape, incest, and sodomy. Additionally, a women's group called *Sauti ya Mama* (Voice of Mothers) was formed, and it is very vocal about these cases. Different parishes have also mobilized their small Christian communities to take an active role in bringing about change in these practices. Outwardly the community is doing more now to protect its children, but other important issues, such as child trafficking, still need to be resolved. There is no current information as to whether the local custom of pregnant mothers permitting husbands to have sex with their daughter(s) has ceased.

Eventually Coralis learned that Lulu's mother had decided not to bring charges against the rapist because he paid her off with $147. She used the money to travel up country for a holiday and to buy Lulu new clothes and shoes. Even though Lulu's mother assured Coralis that part of the money would be used for the child's education, it was small comfort. Because the mother didn't press charges, the rapist went unpunished. As of March 2010, Lulu bore no outward sign of being raped and was doing well in primary school. Despite the fact that Coralis remained vigilant to protect "her" orphans, little did she know at the time that Lulu would propel her to undertake a new ministry, a rescue center for children trafficked and raped.

Is Suffering Ever Justified?

Father Nicky Hennity, another Kiltegan priest, is co-pastor with Father Gabe Dolan of the newly built St. Patrick's Church in Bangala, another large Mombasa slum. Like Gabe, Nicky speaks with a pronounced Irish accent. He has served in East Africa as a missionary for over thirty-two years. He was in Rwanda for twelve years, right after the ceasefire that ended the genocide, and he has been in Kenya for a total of twenty years. Unlike Gabe, whose physical presence and mannerisms bespeak authority, Nicky is soft spoken, pensive, and reflective. They are truly an "odd couple" as they passionately represent the poor.

Coralis works closely with both Gabe and Nicky, since many of the project's orphans and guardians live in Bangala. Over the years, they have become not only colleagues, but good friends who inspire her with their missionary zeal. Generally, the foreign missionary community spends holidays and other celebrations, both spiritual and social, together. In the absence of her own family and children, this small nucleus of friends quickly became her family.

What does blessed are the poor mean for Nicky? He responds, "There is no way we can bless institutional poverty. The poor are the signs that our world is not working. Institutional poverty results from a system that has failed the poor. Luke's Jesus means, 'blessed are the poor with spirit' because their spirit has not been broken; they want to work, they want to educate their children, they want to rise to leadership. In contrast, in many of the slums like Bangala, people's spirits have been broken when the only way they can see out of the poverty is drugs, alcohol, crime, or prostitution."

"There are two distinct socioeconomic groups here— those 'poor with spirit' and those 'poor without spirit.' They are both a big challenge to Christ's message. There is no good news for the 'poor without spirit.' You can't say that they are going to be rewarded in the next life because the kingdom of God is here and now. The message is that we have failed to bring the kingdom into a reality, and this is a real challenge. On the other hand, the 'poor with spirit' live in the moment with hope and determination that their lives will make a difference for their children, and that is their blessing."

"In the story of Exodus, God 'heard the cry of the poor.'" Hennity said. "We have a God who hears the cry of the poor and has given us the tools and resources to reduce the poverty and suffering of poor people. We have the power, the 'light and the salt' to give to the people. God is listening to their cry. At Calvary when Christ was stripped naked, he called out, 'My God, my God, why have you abandoned me?' God is with the poor because Christ died on Calvary a poor, abandoned person."

According to Nicky, service to the poor requires two essential abilities. The first is the ability to determine what is needed in a given situation to help the people, and the second is giving them the right resources to handle the situation. "We are the light to show them. For now, what we can do for the poor is to give them the knowledge and skills to handle situations such as small projects, to provide nursery schools and primary schools, and to offer microloans for small businesses so people can see a slight improvement, however slow their progress. We who minister to the poor have to get our own perspective right or we will just give up. . . . We must do little things and do them well," he says.

Does Nicky believe that poverty, with its degrading human conditions and the AIDS pandemic, can be successfully resolved? He responds, "There are immense riches in Africa. Just look at the rich people who live next to the slums. This is the great contradiction of Africa: there is an immense wealth here alongside the greatest poverty. We have to try to eliminate the poverty, which will take many years, and we will have to do it slowly. The Christian theme is to use one's life to make a difference. It is humiliating to have minor results, but when you look at the cross, what do you see? Total humiliation, Christ stripped naked. The whole theology of the cross is a positive theology that gives us a great hope that there is resurrection in the midst of suffering."

The message of suffering and resurrection replays itself every day in Coralis's work, and she has struggled with that reality throughout her ministry. She observes that "suffering surrounds us. It seems to be a partner in life, like day and night, up and down, and high and low. Demonizing suffering does not help. Recognizing it as a part of life that calls us to reach out to others should bring about an inner change in us." Coralis's perspective on suffering and poverty demands that she and all other people ask themselves what they are doing to make a difference. Leonardo Boff, a liberation theologian, articulated this very clearly.

> God does not explain why there is suffering—God suffers alongside us. God does not explain why there is sorrow—God became the man of sorrows. God does not explain why there is humiliation—God empties himself. We are no longer alone in our vast loneliness. God is with us. We are no longer in solitude, but rather in solidarity. The arguments from reason are silenced. It is the heart that speaks. It tells the story of a God who became a child, who did not ask questions but who acts, who does not offer explanations but lives out an answer.[1]

Thus, there is really no justification or rational answer to the question of why all this suffering exists. It appears

---

[1] Leonardo Boff, *The Path to Hope: Fragments from a Theologian's Journey* (Maryknoll, NY: Orbis Books, 1993), 91.

that all that can be said—which really makes little sense—is that we "live our lives to make a difference," as does Mrs. Mugo, Felisita, Chizi, Winnie, Nicky, Gabe, Emmah, Coralis, Juliana, and a myriad of others as they accompany and walk with the poor. Our human intellect can explain only so much, and the rest simply remains a mystery.

For Nicky and Coralis, the real challenge to Christ's message is the actual events of each day, the reality of brutal poverty and of people dying before their time. During Lent in 2010, Nicky and Gabe, who are both over fifty, undertook an ambitious project of visiting every one of the five hundred or so "houses" (actually mud shanties for the most part) in Bangala to offer a blessing, no matter the faith belief of the families.

Susan had walked through the Bangala slum with Coralis as they distributed treated malaria nets to AIDS families. The climate is hot and humid and the air foul smelling. The hilly, rocky earth is dotted with vast gullies and gorges caused by heavy rain. Sometimes shanties collapse, killing the families within. Nicky commented that "these shanties, no matter how sparse, are people's homes. It's not the mansions of the rich, but these mud huts are still their palaces. By blessing the houses and the people, we are telling them that they are precious in the eyes of God and that God loves them. Christ identified with the poor himself. By the visits, we get to the reality that we live with the poor and the poor reflect the presence of Christ in a real way. The institutional church prefers a sacramental Christ because it's less demanding. We spend an hour in church on Sunday and that's it. It's much more difficult to spend an hour under the roof of someone who is really poor. That person is more real. That poor person is the real presence of Christ."

Susan asked Nicky whether he thought God might be sad at the state of events in so many countries in the Global South. Nicky smiled, quietly laughed, and then quickly responded that he would not presume to speak for God. However, he said, "From a human point of view, we can certainly say that God is sad. For example, at the death of Lazarus, there were tears in Jesus' eyes. So the tears are probably still flowing from the eyes of God, which is a challenge to us. We should be motivated to do something about it."

(Coralis Salvador)

Susan on a home visit to distribute malaria nets to
pregnant women and sick patients in the slums of Mombasa.

Postelection Violence

Nancy Adhiambo, twenty-two years old, has a broad, illuminating smile. Her quiet spirit exudes joy and radiance in a calm, self-assured manner. She has a soft-spoken voice, and even the harsh scars of severe burns that mar her neck and her arms become seemingly invisible when she speaks about her faith. Nancy never knew her parents. From infancy, she had been raised by an aunt who had AIDS. After one year of assistance from the AIDS Orphans' Project, her aunt died, leaving her homeless at fifteen years of age. With no identifiable family left, nor the possibility of a guardian, Coralis placed Nancy in a boarding high school. During school breaks, she stayed with her late aunt's neighbor in exchange for doing household chores.

In December 2007, after finishing high school and without telling Coralis, Nancy left Mombasa and traveled alone up country to explore whatever family roots she could find in Kisumu. Shortly after connecting with her mother's side of the family, she realized that these relatives were simply too poor to take her in or offer assistance, and she decided to return to Mombasa to pursue her dream of higher education. Tragically, before she left Kisumu Nancy became a victim of the postelection tribal violence between the Kikuyus and the Luo tribes.

Since Kenyan independence in 1964, the country's leaders have come primarily from the Kikuyu tribe. However, their inefficient and corrupt governments have caused great resentment among the other tribes who naturally felt disenfranchised. In the 2007 general election, President Kibaki, a Kikuyu, ran for reelection against the main opposition party candidate, Raila Odinga, a member of the Luo tribe.

The election was rife with corruption, and the people re-acted violently when the Electoral Commission of Ke-nya proclaimed that President Kibaki had a margin that was larger than the total number of possible voters. The people reacted to such corruption with protests and dem-onstrations that escalated into violence, mass murders, and the enormous destruction of property. Over two hundred thousand people were displaced as competing tribes tore through formerly peaceful neighborhoods, forcing neigh-bors of other tribes to leave. More than one thousand peo-ple were killed, countless women and girls were raped, and others were mutilated. A fragile peace was finally brokered by former UN Secretary General Kofi Annan. Unfortu-nately, more than four years later, unrest remains along with a serious mistrust on the part of the population toward its government. To date, there have been no prosecutions of the criminals implicated in the rampages.

Nancy described her attack by a neighbor. "She took a large, boiling cauldron of tea and for no reason, hurled it at me, hitting my face and upper body, and then she ran away. I've never seen her to this day." Nancy suffered major burns on her neck, arms, and torso. She received minimal medi-cal treatment, in reality, simply an herbal salve prepared by the local medicine man. Incredibly, as she retold her story, she bore no anger or malice toward her assailant. She said, "I thank God that I am okay now!" After eighteen months of recuperation, Nancy finally contacted Coralis, who was enormously relieved. She'd been thinking all sorts of awful things might have happened. Perhaps Nancy had been mar-ried off by her relatives to gain a dowry price, or raped, or trafficked into prostitution. With Coralis's assistance, Nan-cy enrolled in a Montessori teachers' training school in

Mombasa. She will soon become the first graduate of the AIDS Project to become a teacher.

Nancy displayed a quiet, yet courageous sadness when she reflected on the loss of her parents when she was so young. "I don't even have their images; I don't know what they looked like. I was brought up by my aunt, and since her death I've stayed with former neighbors or anyone who felt like taking me in." Explaining the situation of being an AIDS orphan in a boarding school, she said she had experienced many challenges, especially during visiting days when other students' parents came with snacks for their children. With no family ever coming to visit her, Nancy felt quite alone.

Without the safety net of a loving family, Nancy recounts that it was her belief in God that kept her motivated and focused during her boarding-school years. "I know that God is there for everybody and even if nobody is visiting me, I know that God is visiting me spiritually. I knew that I am from a poor family because even the clothes that I have to put on I've received from Coralis who collects clothes for the orphans from anyone willing to give. On vacations from school, I had nowhere to go. I would go to the homes of my friends, and they would welcome me for the vacation until I finished my secondary school."

Nancy's remarkable faith and confidence in God did not come without some occasional doubt, which is only natural for someone so young. "Yes, I have questioned God. I asked where God was during these times. Yes, I got angry with God. I do not know why this happened to me. In fact, I don't know why my parents died. I don't know why I don't have a place to stay. I don't know where I'm supposed to look for my food and clothes. I don't know why my parents are not here to help me. I still don't have an answer, but I am happy that I have faith in God. I trust in God and I know that with God, everything is possible!"

What does blessed are the poor mean for Nancy? The blessing "speaks to poor people who have nothing, not even a place to stay. I feel blessed because I had somebody to get me to school and give me clothes and food, even bringing me snacks when I was in boarding school. I feel blessed because I have somebody who cares for me like Mama Coralis. She is a blessing from God, and it is God who has brought her to help us. She has taken me from primary school when my parents were not there. She has taken me to boarding school so I could finish high school. She has done everything for me and I am very grateful about her."

A Place of Respite

The constant and incessant all-enveloping poverty in the Global South can be very difficult for a Western missioner to comprehend. For the Maryknoll Lay Missioners, Coralis's sponsoring organization, the safety of missioners is of paramount importance. Over the years a number of lay women and men have been murdered or raped. Others have suffered from mental or physical breakdowns and contracted malaria or other diseases. This is the reality of mission work. Although danger is sometimes unavoidable, the organization does not want its missioners to live in unsafe locations. In theory, their home in the host country should be a respite from the stress of their daily work. Coralis lived her entire stay in a simple flat in the Muslim section of Mombasa that she shared with other missioners. It was relatively comfortable even though she shared the flat with multiple mosquitoes, insects, lizards, black crows, and the occasional baboon outside the windows. She hand washed her own laundry in a bucket in the shower well.

Coralis also found a place of respite in the community of Mivumoni on the south coast, another site of her ministry. In Mivumoni the people had a source of water, they owned small farms, and most of them had known each other since birth. The tranquil existence in this farming community was in stark contrast to the brutality of the slums of Mombasa where people were thrown together, haphazardly and by circumstance, as a result of poverty and the AIDS pandemic. In Mivumoni, by contrast, Coralis witnessed the African way of living that is grounded in sharing, in unity, and in the interdependency of all creation, including the ancestors, from birth to one's final destination. The people uphold family values, the values of community, and the role of elders. Parents work on their small farms growing corn, coconuts, fruit, mangos, cashews, and green oranges, and they raise goats, sheep, chickens, and cows for milk. The children go to school and participate regularly in their mosque or church. Mivumoni was, for Coralis, always an oasis from life in the slums.

Mivumoni is a trek from Mombasa that requires waiting for perhaps hours on the ferry line, with the loud background noise of the *matatu tout* (conductor) screaming the destination, "Ferry, ferry, ferry." Throngs of people, Muslims and Christians, as well as cars, large container trucks, bicycles, and pushcarts laden with all sorts of produce wait patiently to board the ferry that crosses over this inlet of the Indian Ocean to Likoni on the south coast. The *matatus* are a chaotic mode of public transport. A driver, wearing a blue shirt, and a fare collector, dressed

in a burgundy shirt, stands at the open sliding door plat-
form on the side of the *matatu*, yelling out the intended
location. Very calmly the passengers get on, climbing over
other passengers as they try to squeeze into an available
seat. The crowd always includes mothers with babies
strapped on their backs, veiled women, and perhaps a few
chickens in a crate, with a mattress or sometimes a wood
coffin containing a body on top of the *matatu*.

Once the ferry docks, there's a frenzied rush as the people and vehicles try to exit onto a one-lane road. In reality, everyone waits long periods of time in the sweltering
African heat. While waiting, cars and trucks idle, spewing
noxious fumes, and a procession of street vendors bang on
the cars, holding aloft recently caught fish or live chickens,
murky water repackaged in semiclean plastic bottles, nuts,
t-shirts, or flip flops. The ever-present beggars, street children, and prostitutes also crowd about. While waiting to
egress the ferry, people sit in their cars and sweat. You can
also do a week's shopping!

The majority of the people in Mivumoni are from the
Kamba tribe. The tribal characteristics include intact family
units and strong community relationships. They are hardworking, and their main source of income is tied to the
earth. Kamba farmers raise chickens, goats, and cows in very
fertile land made up of brick red earth and rolling hills. At
dusk during the planting season, one can stand at a high
point and gaze down at Shimba Hills and enjoy the glow
of the huge, red orange sun setting. Shortly afterwards, small
isolated and controlled fires ignited to clear the land dot
the entire panoramic view. Mivumoni helped Coralis stay
deeply connected to what she witnessed as "another reality of Kenya." The people were unlike those in other areas

where she served. Each Mivumoni visit renewed her, so she tried to go two to three times each month.

Father Joseph Kengah, a Mombasa diocesan priest, began his pastoral ministry in Mivumoni and its seven outstations in 1997. Joe is a very compassionate and caring pastor, and he and Coralis have developed a special symbiotic relationship, tackling very difficult and seemingly insurmountable projects on behalf of the people they serve. Two of their many collaborations include an epilepsy clinic in Mivumoni and the idea to create a secondary school for the deaf. Their incredibly effective partnership includes everything from transporting European and American donors from the airport to the parish center to Tsavo, the famous national park located west of Mombasa, to finding opportunities for educational sponsorship for the youths. They are tireless in these endeavors. Joe, who is the epitome of calm in this land of teeming chaos, is frequently sought out by parishioners, colleagues, missioners, and clergy to help come up with innovative solutions to their many problems. He tackles each challenge, with seemingly effortless ease and compassion, and couches every solution with the sentiment *Hakuna matata* (no problem), even though, in reality, he is attempting to move the proverbial mountain.

Even though Mivumoni was Coralis's great escape to tranquility, it also provided some of the scariest and most fearful times of her mission life. Joe had taught her how to drive a stick shift, four-wheel drive vehicle in this rugged terrain. He also showed her how to analyze the roadbeds when coming across flooded areas, bush, and fallen trees. He even showed her how to detect if the soil would hold the weight of a car.

Once, travelling to Mivumoni alone, Coralis got caught in a maze of the terrifying unknown. As the roadbed was flooded, she couldn't pass through and instead turned around and took the longer forest route. She knew there were wild boars, buffalo, baboons, and, most fearful to her, snakes. There was also no cell phone connection, no way back, with only the forest beyond and her mounting fear. As she gunned the engine through the forest path, praying out loud to calm herself, tall African grass and baby palm trees laden with heavy flat leaves slapped against the car. Exiting the forest, back to familiar territory, she exhaled in relief. She later noticed that the caked mud on the belly of the vehicle had been brushed clean from the forests' overgrowth, and she smiled.

Transporting foreign donors also had inherent peril. Most of them expected to be escorted to the national park of Tsavo. Joe and Coralis had the two-day overnight trip down pat. Coralis packed the thermos of *chai* tea, lunches, drinks, and snacks, and she made the overnight reservations. Joe fueled the pickup truck and made sure the wooden benches for the picnic were in the back. Nighttime in Tsavo is coal black, and the silence is broken only by the sound of night creatures, but Joe and Coralis were well aware that the park closed at 6:00 p.m., and they knew exactly when and where to exit. However, a donor's request was not to be ignored.

As dusk approached, with the burnt orange and rust African sky layered beneath a golden haze, the donor, looking at a map, pointed to a road she wanted to travel en route to the exit gate. Joe and Coralis were unfamiliar with the route, but Joe wanted to please the donor. Coralis recounts the adventure: "We went through several patches of flooded road with no problem. When we approached what looked like a much bigger flood, we hesitated. Joe looked for signs of tire tracks. We tried to cross and got hopelessly stuck in a deep bed of mud. As Joe got out to assess the situation, I jumped into the driver's side. As darkness fell he sunk up to his knees in mud and animal dung, and I panicked. I was terrified that the 'big five' (lions, elephants, zebras, giraffes, and buffalo) plus snakes would smell us and pounce from the dark abyss. I was also really ticked off at Joe for allowing the donor to overrule his common sense. I was screaming at Joe as he went into the bush to get heavy rocks to put under the tires. I got even angrier because he was going so slowly. Since the donor refused to get out and help, Joe and I switched places. He was a better driver to get us out, and I could collect the boulders a lot faster. I yelled at the donor to be the "lookout." At that point I was in mud and dung, barefoot, up to my thighs, grabbing boulders as fast as I could and shoving them in front of the rear tires. Malaria-carrying mosquitoes swarmed around my sweaty body. No amount of insect repellant would keep them off their intended target. Every time Joe gunned the gas, I was showered with another layer of mud. We finally got out, and, thankfully, the donor made up for it by paying for major structural repairs to Joe's church in Mivumoni. As soon as I could, I drew big red XXXXXXs over that road on our Tsavo map."

The Epilepsy Ministry

As Joe became familiar with his parishioners and the different communities, he saw the urgent need to address the plight of children and adults suffering from epilepsy. The major cause of epilepsy was a neglected high fever from a bout of malaria, especially among infants and children. The community didn't understand the nature of epilepsy. They believed in the myth that the condition was brought about by an evil spirit and was a curse or a punishment for sin. Therefore the illness brought great shame to the family, and the condition of the epileptic was carefully hidden. Joe would countenance none of such myths or practice of witchcraft and instead sought to create awareness and a medical solution for the problems of epilepsy.

When Coralis first arrived in Mombasa, she was assigned to work in the parish of Mivumoni. Under Joe's leadership, she learned how to run an epilepsy clinic, and the parishioners, villagers, and students in the surrounding schools were taught about the condition. When the clinic began in January 2002, it was simply an "add-on" to the already existing dispensary. But Coralis and Joe hired trained staff and a clinic officer. Then a regular clinic day for epileptics was held on the second Friday of each month to assess patients and supply them with a month of medication.

Because of this awareness campaign in schools and different communities, over time people were no longer fearful if a child or neighbor had a seizure. They had been educated on how to handle the situation, and over time the previous stigmatization lessened. More patients began coming to the clinic and to Coralis's surprise, even children who had learned about epilepsy in school were able to identify epilepsy in their mother or other members of the family and accompany them to the clinic.

When asked to relate the situation that gave her the greatest joy in mission, Coralis movingly tells the story of Muthoka, a four-year-old, malnourished boy with epilepsy who developed an enlarged head because of a brain tumor.

As an infant, Muthoka had contracted epilepsy after a bout of malaria and was in desperate need of brain surgery. What next enfolded for Coralis and this family were the extraordinary circumstances that allowed them to rescue this boy. There were no funds to support Muthoka's needs outside the epilepsy clinic, especially for the critically needed brain surgery. Coralis happened to meet a knowledgeable and kind-hearted doctor from the Aga Khan Hospital, a prominent medical facility in Mombasa, and a CAT scan confirmed that the boy needed brain surgery. Unfortunately, no doctor in Mombasa was specialized enough to perform the delicate surgery. Inexplicably, a team of brain surgeons from Nairobi were scheduled to be in Mombasa the week after Muthoka had his CAT scan. The doctor who had initially diagnosed the boy agreed to arrange the surgery at Coast General, a government hospital, with the visiting team of surgeons. He advised Coralis that she should be prepared to pay about $2,000 for the cost of the surgery, the operating room, hospitalization, medications, and postoperative treatment.

Coralis and Joe simply did not have the money. Although they knew that the boy would die without the surgery, Coralis refused to accept that Muthoka would die "on her watch." Deep inside she believed that help would come. In fact, in one of those "freak" episodes of her ministry, after she booked the surgery, a friend from Mendocino, California, called her from out of nowhere and asked how she could be of assistance. Coralis described the urgent need to save this child. The donor immediately sent $2,000, and Muthoka underwent successful surgery. As it turned out, the visiting surgeons donated their services at no cost after learning of the boy's family situation.

*Four-year-old Muthoka being carried by his
mother before his brain surgery for epilepsy.*

Muthoka was hospitalized for thirty-eight days. Every day Coralis visited him, bringing needed medicine and providing meals and money for his mother who stayed with him in the hospital the entire time. After almost a year of recovery and therapy to regain his movements and speech, Muthoka was able to start kindergarten. He is now ten years old and is doing quite well in Class 2 in a special educational program in a Shimba Hills school. Coralis beams brightly when retelling Muthoka's miraculous story. "The Lord always hears the cry of the poor when we are willing to be God's partner."

Chapter 5

Blessed Are Those
Who Are Poor but Hardworking

The Importance of Catholic Social Teaching

One of the best kept secrets of the Catholic Church is its social teaching, a set of values that permeates the very foundation of its vision of the gospel message. Time and time again Jesus of Nazareth preached social justice and compassion for all people, especially the downtrodden, sounding much like the prophets of the Hebrew Scriptures. Because of his concern for the poor and outcasts, some people called him an "agitator" or regarded him as a revolutionary. Based on the gospel message, Catholic social teaching integrates the principles of inclusion, solidarity, faith, and the dignity of all people. Followers of Jesus are challenged not only to believe but to walk the talk.

In the twenty-first century, faced with the reality of climate change and an increasing degradation of the environment, a much greater emphasis is being placed on stewardship of the Earth. We human beings are entrusted with the responsibility to care for the integrity of the Earth so that it will be preserved for future generations. Even in this area, Catholic social teaching provides a roadmap. It includes a vision of the world that celebrates the interconnectedness of all humanity, creation, and the universe.

An integral part of Catholic social teaching, the dignity of all people, demands that missioners first listen to the community in their host country. What are the needs of the people? How can the people participate in meeting these needs? What are their rights and responsibilities? The AIDS Orphans' Project followed these principles of Catholic social teaching. It was the youths who identified their need for their own support groups, which gave rise to workshops such as Education for Life and Adventures Unlimited. In the broader church-sponsored program of Justice and Peace, community leaders known as animators identify current issues affecting the community.

One immediately identified area of need throughout Africa has been the AIDS pandemic. The official response of the Catholic Church toward the pandemic in Africa has been heroic in one sense and extremely controversial in another. The U.S.-based Catholic Relief Services (CRS), Caritas (the German branch), and CAFOD (the UK branch) have long been in the forefront of providing medicine, food, and financial support for administrative costs as well as training for staff, health-care workers, and care-givers. All goods and services are provided without regard to religious affiliation or ethnicity.

The Catholic Church received public criticism in March 2009 when Pope Benedict XVI made his first visit to the African continent. His comments raised concerns on the part of health-care workers trying to halt the spread of AIDS when he declared that condoms were not the answer in the fight against HIV/AIDS. The pontiff expressed his belief that condoms could make the problem worse and that only sexual abstinence and fidelity would prevent the disease from spreading. The pope's approach divided clergy and others working with AIDS patients on the front lines of the battle.

Compassion is a cornerstone of Catholic social teaching. The value of human life and the common good is paramount. Coralis, and many other professionals, including some in the church hierarchy in Mombasa, believe that preserving life is most important. Thus, they counsel the youths on issues of human sexuality, including the various methods of contraception, believing that saving lives is most important.

Liberation Theology and the Option for the Poor

Jesus' message as portrayed in the four gospels is clear and unequivocal, and his disciples are called to follow him. It was to the poor, whom he called blessed, that he promised the kingdom of God and salvation. According to the Gospel of Matthew, serving the poor implies service to Christ himself (15:40–45). This includes the radical demand to give not only alms and share what one has, but also to give oneself and to become poor through love for the poor. Father Nicky Hennity, copastor of St. Patrick's in the Bangala slum, sums it up this way: "The Christian theme is to use our lives to make a difference." This was also Coralis's reality for nearly a decade.

Liberation theology, with its emphasis on an option for the poor, developed in Latin America in the late 1960s. It was a response to God's call in Exodus to "let my people go" and directed a brilliant light on the struggle of the marginalized poor. It eventually spread to other impoverished countries in the Global South, including Kenya. Like Catholic social teaching, liberation theology always starts with the given reality. What's going on in the real lives of the people on the ground? In a way, it can be said to be a bottom-up view of life, as liberation theology focuses on what the Hebrew Scriptures and New Testament have to say about those people who are looked upon as nonhuman beings. Those who are poor, suffering, abused, in pain and need, and grieving over loss are challenged to become God's partners in hearing the cry of the poor. This new way of doing theology challenges the nonpoor to act.

The poor have a sacred place in Catholic social teaching, liberation theology, and in God's eye not because they are necessarily better than other people, but because they are poor and living in conditions contrary to God's will. The basis for their privileged position is the universality of God's love. All are able to be in solidarity with those who suffer wretched conditions and oppression, and whom the social order ignores and exploits. Gustavo Gutiérrez of Peru, known as the father of liberation theology, argues that there is a scriptural basis for this option for the poor. Reading the Scriptures from the perspective of the poor, two primary themes stand out: the universality and gratuity of God's love, and God's preferential option for the poor. If God's love is universal and given freely and equally to all, and God's love has been made manifest in our human history filled with injustice, conflict, and division, then God's love must take sides with the victims of that injustice, conflict, and division, and the victims are usually the marginalized poor.[1]

---

[1] Gustavo Gutiérrez, *A Theology of Liberation* (Maryknoll, NY: Orbis Books, 1995), 175.

(Maryknoll Mission Archives/Sean Sprague)

Chizi with her five orphaned grandchildren.

In response to the need to be close to the people, each Catholic parish in Kenya includes groups of small Christian communities (SCCs). Comprised of children, teens, adults, and the elderly, the SCCs are the lifeblood of the larger church. All of the AIDS Project health-care volunteers come from the SCCs. These volunteers who identify potential clients and orphans are indispensable to the project because they live among the people, developing relationships with them and monitoring their situations. They are concerned with the welfare of the community, and they also take an active role in keeping the church alive and vibrant and growing.

The Justice and Peace Program

The Justice and Peace programs of the Catholic Church in Kenya came about to address people's basic human rights, community problems, and the AIDS pandemic. Based on Catholic social teaching, the curriculum deals with a wide range of abuses. A specific problem is the nature of Kenya's overwhelmingly patriarchal society, which places less emphasis on girls, especially regarding education. In addition, conflicts in the villages surrounding national parks occur when marauding animals escape and rampage the villages, destroying precious crops and killing people. Land grabbing by corrupt government officials also occurs, as happened both before and after the 2007 national election.

During the colonial period throughout Africa, the British, the French, and the other colonial powers, including elected officials, claimed the most fertile land, and many landowners in Kenya still hold titles to land that was illegitimately obtained. By contrast, the vast majority of Kenyans are landless squatters. International companies, with the consent of the government, prey upon the powerless, forcing their relocation so the companies can extract precious minerals. They rarely give fair compensation in exchange. The police themselves are often corrupt, and the justice system seems unable or unwilling to cope with this multitude of human rights abuses.

Recently, Justice and Peace programs in the Global South have expanded to include an "integrity of creation" component. As noted above, in addition to basic human rights, emphasis is now being placed on the abundance of the Earth's resources and the necessity that they must be enjoyed and shared by all peoples and not simply exploited and extracted by the nonpoor of the Global North.

In Mombasa, Emmah Ndonye, a Justice and Peace fieldworker, and Father Gabe Dolan, the program's chaplain, engage daily with the community on these issues. Sometimes their efforts work beautifully, and other times they fall on deaf ears. In the fall of 2006, Susan and Emmah traveled together throughout Emmah's "territory." Emmah refuses to spoon-feed or pamper the people. She understands her job to be one of empowering and educating the people to stand up for themselves. On one occasion Susan and Emmah took a *matatu* to visit the community of Aldina in the Mikindani area, west of Mombasa. After they "alighted" on the main road, they walked down a very steep path in a hilly area, passing mud huts, with lots of children playing outside, and pathways with pools of murky water. At the bottom of the hill was a riverbed, and it was low tide. As the children kept calling out *mzungu* (foreigner or white person), it was obvious that the only way to cross the muddy flat was to gingerly step on a few cement bags strategically placed across the riverbed. Some disappeared before their eyes as they slipped into the quicksand-like mud.

They finally arrived in Aldina village where the chief and elders, all men, were seated waiting for them. Susan and Emmah observed the customary formal greetings, shaking hands with each person. Emmah then invited community members to voice their concerns. The first thing the elders said was that there was no footbridge across the muddy riverbed and that their children had to make the crossing twice daily to get to and from school. Emmah firmly reminded them that this was her second visit to discuss the need for a footbridge. During the first visit, she had urged the community to organize and to come up with a solution. Now she asked what they had done in the meantime to accomplish this goal. The elders and some younger members immediately said they were *waiting* for an NGO (nongovernmental organization) or a minister of Parliament to provide a bridge. It appeared that they had done absolutely nothing except wait for a handout. Susan carefully surveyed this able-bodied group of men, none of whom seemed to have jobs. The chief, who was wrapped in a bright *kanga* of brilliantly colored fabric with striking patterns, was hearty looking. The assistant chief was a relatively young man, and the ten or twelve others, sitting in a semicircle on plastic chairs, were all obviously physically able to work. In the distance Susan saw an elevated water well powered by electricity. This was a far cry from most of the other villages where the only water sources were dirty pools of rain water. It turned out that an NGO had built the well.

Emmah quickly lost her patience and raised her voice to a booming pitch: "Why has nothing been done about this footbridge?" She then looked down at her feet, raised them up a bit so everyone could see them, surveyed the men with a long, hard glare, and declared louder than before, "And why are my shoes still muddy?" Susan was flabbergasted at the tone of Emmah's voice. Susan looked down at her muddy sandals as the men sheepishly responded with inept attempts to solicit sympathy. But Emmah would have none of it. She was not interested in working on behalf of those who wanted handouts. She wanted to spend her time with the active poor, those poor and hardworking who were willing to work alongside her.

The concepts of the poor with dignity and the poor with spirit were apparent in the Bangala slum on Palm Sunday in 2010. Coralis and Susan wanted to be part of the procession to mass at St. Patrick's. They were told the procession would begin on the outskirts of the slum. Arriving, they looked across the dusty roadway swarming with trucks and *matatus* and saw two processions, not sure which one was theirs. Susan pointed to one and jumped to the immediate conclusion that since it had the most participants in regal-looking vestments and pomp, it must include the Catholics, but she was wrong. Although regal and colorful, that procession was from a segment of former Catholics who had broken away from the Catholic Church and permitted its priests, sisters, and bishops to marry. Naturally this puts them at odds with the Vatican.

They headed over to the other procession and found Father Nicky Hennity, wearing simple vestments, surrounded by people singing and swaying palms. They noticed how meticulous everyone was: the children were dressed in pristine, clean, pressed dresses and white shirts, pants, and shoes. Women and men were in traditional garb or Western clothes. The choir wore matching *kanga* shirts or skirts, and a number of people wore sashes printed with the name of the church. Inside the church, there was standing room only.

A Catholic mass in Africa is usually long and may take around two hours, with traditional ancestral music and much singing and dancing. The Bangala congregation was characterized by dignity and a deep spirituality. The priest was but a minor participant in the celebration. Children and youths were baptized; church elders, women and men, appealed for funds to support their church; and the music and dancing was energetic and infectious. These proud people, the suffering servants of the slums, some of whom Susan had already visited to deliver malaria nets, could have fit into any church on the fabled north shore of Long Island.

They were proud and dignified, and they finally had a parish and a beautiful church to call their own. Later that year they also funded a nursery school and a dispensary. Some of these Bangala people were poor but hardworking, poor but dignified, and poor but determined. They did not wait for a handout to achieve their dreams.

Nonetheless, there are also some people in Bangala, like the Aldina elders, who want handouts. Coralis sighs, "It's never a perfect situation. There will always be a certain percentage who don't want to work. I have seen that in my microfinance projects, in the epilepsy clinic, and among guardians of the AIDS Project. They are not all like Felisita and Chizi. These people continue to be our challenge—how can we motivate them to empower themselves?"

Moving On

In 2007, as she neared the end of her second three-year contract, Coralis began to grow restless. At times she thought out loud that perhaps it was time for her to move on to another missionary assignment. She was committed to continuing the work but felt that the AIDS Orphans' Project and the epilepsy clinic were up and running and could be turned over to another lay missioner or to the Kenyans themselves. Even a new challenge to help Father Joe build the first secondary school for the deaf in the coastal region was not sufficient to quell her unbounded energy and restlessness. However, the challenge of creating awareness of the plight of the deaf and raising funds to build the school was a huge undertaking. They planned a walk along the coast of 150 miles, from the border of Tanzania in the south to the northern coast of Malindi. There were only three secondary schools for the deaf in all of Kenya, and all were located in the western part of the country. Compounding the problem was the fact that culturally, the disabled, especially children, are some of the most neglected members of Kenyan society. This is true generally throughout Africa. The challenge of this project certainly interested her, and of equal importance was Joe's motivation since two of his eight siblings had been born deaf. But would this be enough to keep Coralis in Mombasa?

In Maryknoll circles, the time-honored definition of a missionary is someone who goes where they are not wanted but needed, and then leaves when they are not needed but wanted. These thoughts rattled around in Coralis's head. "Where did God want her to go next?" she wondered. After seven years in Kenya, her understanding of mission was "to know, love, and serve God. To serve as Jesus asks us to do, to bring God's kingdom here and now." To serve means dying to one's own self-interest. "You let go, you give up your pride, your sense of power, control, and security and allow God's will to come through. In mission, it is amazing that at the end of the day, in spite of physical exhaustion, you are satisfied and energized by God's joy and you find your heart is full!"

Coralis left for home leave in California in the summer of 2007. This gave her time to reflect on where God was leading her. In Mombasa, a plan was already in place to establish a rescue center for young girls and boys who had been raped, trafficked, or lured into prostitution. Such a center interested Coralis because she had witnessed so many of her orphans undergoing these ordeals. Even though the AIDS Project had increased in dimension, evolving into a holistic program of care, it was still not equipped to deal with the issues confronting these children. She was greatly challenged by this opportunity.

God and Politics:
Building the Well and the Rescue Center

In 2007, Susan returned to the United States from her short-term volunteer assignment in Kenya. She and Coralis had become good friends. Susan felt blessed to have her as a mentor. When they put their heads together, they felt unstoppable. Little did they envision that they would both experience challenges in their faith due to projects they undertook.

Clean, potable water is sorely lacking in Kenya. This very basic human right struck a chord in Susan. She requested that a community be identified that was in need of a well for water. The diocesan water engineer selected Mukundi in the Shimba Hills, a remote area of low-income, small-scale farmers. Since time immemorial, the community's only water source was the Ramisi River in addition to the collection of rainwater in oversized tanks. The river is located about twelve and a half miles from the village. It is the job of the women and girls to trek down the mountain with large yellow jerry cans, draw the water, and travel back up with the cans on their heads. Frequently, the girls miss school because of this time-consuming responsibility. This is also where the women washed their clothes. The river was infested with crocodiles, and approximately ten or twelve villagers were killed every year while drawing water. Also, since 1998 Mukundi had been suffering from a severe drought and had endured numerous conflicts between humans and the abundant wildlife.

Emmah, Coralis, Susan, and a water engineer traveled to Mukundi to meet with the village elders. First they took the ferry toward Likoni and then spent three hours traveling through rugged, mountainous hills over bumpy, rural dirt roads shaded with coconut, mango, and cashew trees. As the main road cuts through a national park reserve, they were thrilled to see water buffalo and elephants up close. They passed numerous small villages with government primary schools and makeshift markets selling clothes, fruits, and vegetables. Slaughtered goats and cows were hanging in the heat. They passed many mosques with white-washed exteriors and Arabic lettering in faded blue or green. Most mosques have a separate entrance for women at the back and a *madrasa*, a religious study center for the children, in a separate annex.

They arrived at a typical village governed as usual by male elders. However, women are the workhorses of the community, and the group was greeted in typical style by about a dozen *mamas* dressed in traditional *kanga*, along with a few men. Barefoot children milled around, dressed in dusty school uniforms of navy blue shorts and faded white shirts. As the greeting of *Jambo* (hello) rang out, Coralis and Susan noticed that a number of the children had ring-shaped spots on their shaven heads. Such spots are a sign of a parasitic disease that comes from washing with contaminated water.

The group, with other members of the community, went into a partially completed church that had a few homemade benches scattered around haphazardly. Large piles of maize were on the cement floor in the back. Members of the village began to talk. Five years before, this group of women had raised funds to have a well dug by hand. The dishonest contractor dug a fake well and then disappeared with all the money. The water engineer pointed out that a geographical survey indicated that a borehole was an option.

During the lengthy visit, they were served *chai* tea and *mandazi*, a local pastry similar to a doughnut but triangular in shape. In addition to the well, the women shared other concerns—the lack of safety for girls harassed by men drunk on the local brew, the infestation of drugs, the lack of a medical facility with not even a clinic in the area. Epilepsy patients had to walk three to four hours each way to get to the clinic in Mivumoni. At the end of the visit, the group of four made no promises, but Susan knew immediately that this is what she wanted to work on. As they said goodbye and before they realized what was happening, the back of their vehicle was loaded with burlap bags full of maize and small, green fruit that looked like limes but turned out to be oranges. This was a gift from the community to show that in their culture visitors are always a blessing. Despite Susan's protestations that they couldn't take food from these villagers who had so little, Coralis explained that they were showing their appreciation, and they graciously accepted the gifts. When Susan returned to New York, she started fund raising for the well, something she had never done before. In the end, getting the funding turned out to be a lot easier than building the actual well. The well was a project that consumed the lives of Coralis and Susan for the next two years.

At the same time, Coralis renewed her contract with the Maryknoll Lay Missioners for another three years and began work on the rescue center and undertook fundraising for a school for the deaf in Kilifi, a village north of Mombasa. This was in addition to overseeing the AIDS

Orphans' Project and the epilepsy clinic. Coralis was working at least six days a week and absolutely thrived on the intensity of her ministry. Eventually she took over the management of the Shimba Hills well once it was discovered that the faith-based organization (FBO) staff charged with the project, the director of development and the water engineer, were both incompetent and corrupt.

While the rescue center was undergoing renovation, Coralis and her colleagues visited the red light district in Mtwapa, located on the north coast of Mombasa. They watched firsthand as young children were being drawn into prostitution. Because this area is close to major national game parks, it has many five-star resorts for the tourists who stay there before and after their safaris. The resorts and safari operators strongly discourage tourists from wandering away from the hotels; however a booming bar and pros-titution center has developed nearby. This is where many children were rescued.

Coralis became the administrator of the center, with a mission statement specifying that it would provide the res-cued kids with a safe environment, board, lodging, counsel-ing, medical treatment, and in-house education. The center made great efforts to prosecute the perpetrators and as-signed social workers to accompany the children for their court appearances. The ultimate goal was to facilitate their reintegration with their birth families, if at all possible. If the family of origin was responsible for the abuse, the cen-ter worked to place the child permanently in a safe alterna-tive setting.

In a short period of time the center was functioning, with forty children supported by an order of religious sisters, social workers, counselors, and other staff. For Coralis, it was like caring for another family all over again. She said, "I needed lots of patience, understanding, and love to share with these new children. The children were traumatized, and their problems were intense and varied. Some children acted out their anger, others were in a world of their own, still others continued to be a challenge both in attitude and behavior, and some simply preferred to remain in seclusion. Those who responded to the counseling and loving care became empowered to be 'big sisters' to the new children arriving almost daily."

Pialine, an eight-year-old AIDS orphan already involved in Coralis's project, was short and skinny and an average student. She had been living with her HIV-positive mother and two younger siblings in an unkempt mud hut in Bomu, another large Mombasa slum area. Pialine's mother sold local brew from their hut and often gave in to the sexual demands of her drunk clients. The mother turned a blind eye when Pialine was repeatedly raped by her mother's boyfriend. Neither Coralis nor the health worker had any idea that the child was being brutally abused. When she was about eleven years old, Pialine screamed out during one such assault and a neighbor intervened. Mrs. Mugo was alerted about the situation and immediately brought Pialine to a government home for children in Kiembeni. She had dropped out of the AIDS Orphans' Project since she was being educated where she had been placed. After a year, she turned up at the rescue center.

Upon admission, the child's physical condition was so deplorable that Coralis did not even recognize her as one of her AIDS orphans. She had grown taller but was obviously malnourished. It was only when Pialine called her "Mama Coralis" that Coralis realized who she was. Stunned by her plight, Coralis broke down and sobbed uncontrollably. "I felt so guilty that I did not follow up with Pialine's case personally while she was in the government home. This child was lifeless; her spirit was broken. She was sad, lost, and forgotten."

As the other children looked on, the reunion of Pialine and Coralis was tearful and heartwarming. This brutalized child had finally been rescued. Coralis knew that she would now be safe and able to begin the healing process. They also brought Pialine's four-year-old sister to the center. Anna had also been molested. After three months of rehabilitation, Pialine sought to be reunited with her family, and efforts were put in place for the reunion, but the mother's continuing prostitution made this impossible. Pialine's mother made no effort to change her behavior and showed no interest in her children. Both girls now live at the center, and it is hoped that they can be moved eventually into the home of a foster family.

Abigail, a seventeen-year-old, was already a mother of an infant named Rose. At seventeen, she was already working as a prostitute when she and her child were rescued. Graceful and statuesque, Abigail was at first quiet and insecure. In a short time, she exhibited much determination to make something of herself for her child. After six months of counseling, rehabilitation, and skills training, both mother and child moved to a rented room in Likoni with support from another organization and began life anew. At last report, Abigail was supporting her little family by operating a small business cooking food. They seemed to be doing quite well.

Back in the United States, in a matter of months Susan was able to raise the money needed for the well. She was stunned both by the amount and the array of donors who heard about the plight of Shimba Hills. Over half of the more than one hundred donors writing checks to a Catholic organization for a well for Muslims and Christians were of the Jewish faith. The well became a truly ecumenical effort. But progress was slow as the development director and the water engineer in Mombasa charged with the implementation of the project gave false reports time and time again and refused to account for where the money went. After a short period of time, both Coralis and Susan knew that something had gone terribly wrong. Susan felt her own spirit begin to deteriorate. She was enraged for the *mamas* of Shimba Hills who never had clean water because of a lack of money. Now the money was in place to build the long-awaited well, but progress was stymied by the corruption on the part of the Kenyan engineer and director. She was outraged at the blatant dishonesty and the utter impotence of their superiors to take any action to investigate and rectify the situation. Church politics, cover-ups, and heavy silence from those in charge forced Susan to dig deeper to fix things for the *mamas* of Shimba Hills. She demanded formal accounting procedures for the donated money and refused to let up. The deceit of the two Kenyan men and their superiors took its toll on her own faith. She ranted to Coralis, via e-mail and phone, about this futile "search for justice," and she found herself asking many times where God could be. Coralis, who was in the center of the storm in Mombasa, was daily questioning the two employees as well as their supervisors. She abandoned typical Kenyan methods and confronted their corruption and ineptitude head on. Coralis promised Susan that she would have the well built "if she had to dig it herself"!

Although Coralis knew absolutely nothing about building water wells, in January 2008 she identified a reputable company to dig a borehole and install a hand pump. Nurseif was a small company owned by two devout Muslims, Seif and his brother Nur. Their great-grandparents had emigrated to Mombasa from the northern part of India in the early 1900s to work as laborers on the British railway being built from the Kenyan port on the Indian Ocean all the way to Uganda. Seif, kind and honest, told Coralis that she would need a permit from the Water Ministry before starting work. Coralis soon discovered that the staff of the FBO assigned to the project (and later fired) never got a copy of the title to the land or the letter of allotment for the site needed for the permit.

So a determined Coralis set about getting the necessary documents from government offices in a bureaucracy fraught with ineptitude. She discovered that the land had been donated by a man named Pius, a Mukundi parishioner. Fortunately he was a catechist at St. Mary's Church, where her AIDS Orphans' Project office is located, and he and Coralis had worked together for a long time, although they were unaware of their Shimba Hills connection. First they went to the Office of Land Mapping to get the identification number of the plot and then they appealed to the Ministry of Land for a copy of the title or a letter of allotment. While generally in Kenya it can take years to get a deed of title, through their dogged persistence, they had all the needed documents in hand in a matter of a few weeks.

Armed with the allotment letter, they filed for a permit to dig, and an engineer from the Water Ministry went with Coralis and Pius to inspect the site. Making the six-hour round trip up the mountains to Shimba Hills became routine. When they reached Mukundi, a group of women waited by the roadside to exuberantly welcome them. They proceeded inside the church and after greetings, prayers, and hymns the meeting began. The women again shared their stories of hardship because of the lack of water. They also shared the story of the previous attempt to dig a well by hand, which they had worked hard to finance before they were cheated by the *fundi* (laborers) and their hard-earned money was gone.

This time things were going to be different. The lawyers, judges, and many others in New York had raised money for a real well. Coralis would right the wrongs of the development director and water engineer of the FBO. The *mamas* were filled with hope that Seif would find water at the depth the survey reported, sixty-two meters down (203 feet). Drilling to such a depth was an incredible challenge in this rocky terrain. As they contemplated having their own well, the women's group discussed the care of the well and the distribution of the future water. With the permit assured, Coralis and the women broke into singing and dancing in jubilation. Gifted with fresh coconuts and other fruits, the visitors returned to Mombasa.

Upon her return to Mombasa, Coralis immediately told Seif that the permit was granted, and steps were taken to begin the dig. Once more they returned to the site so he could assess the location and evaluate what equipment was required. Again they received the same exuberant welcome. Seif instructed the women about the usage and upkeep of the well and the responsibilities entailed in its maintenance. The *mamas* had already formed a water committee to supervise administration, maintenance, and distribution. They planned to collect a small fee for water that would be used for future repairs and maintenance expenses. Seif requested they provide his *fundi* with a steady supply of water for the duration of the project. This was necessary for the drilling process. He also asked them to look for one young, healthy white, unblemished goat, which he paid for, to be slaughtered prior to starting the dig. This was both an appeasement and appreciation gift for their ancestors who had lived on the land from the beginning of time. After the ceremony, the goat was roasted and enjoyed by all.

The following week Seif and his team of ten *fundi,* who would camp out at the site, traveled to Shimba Hills with a borehole-drilling rig. The heavy equipment made the journey even more arduous. The elongated, huge rig was mounted on a trailer bed for the ferry crossing to Likoni and then began the long climb up the mountain on heavily rutted, winding dirt roads. The project was beset with problems from the beginning. First, the trailer broke down due to the roughness of the terrain. Then once the digging began, the unyielding rocks broke the main hammer. The original surveyor's report had been inaccurate in its assessment of the type of rock found. Equipment had to be taken back to Mombasa for repair or replacement. A second hole had to be dug when one of the hammers became embedded at thirty meters and could not be removed.

When she wasn't working at the rescue center or with her orphans, Coralis traveled back and forth to the site. As the problems mounted, she "thanked God for providing Seif, a fine man, committed to the work, who persevered. He told me that this was the longest time he had spent digging a borehole. He wondered if 'forces' were against them." In the end, the community brought in several local religious leaders—Muslims, Christians, and tribal elders—to pray and bless the well.

Seif had reached the sixty-meter level but still hadn't found water. "I was very stressed and anxious," says Coralis. "According to our contract, if no water was reached by sixty-two meters, the digging would stop, and the funds raised by Susan would have been wasted. Susan never knew about the problems and simply believed that once I took over, the well would be completed." As the drilling slowly progressed, Coralis's mind went wild, creating all types of scenarios as to what would happen if the project died. "But I trusted in God and the words 'Do not let your heart be troubled' took over." Finally, on April 15, 2008, one of the spiritual readings at the daily mass was from the Acts of the Apostles: "Look, there is water!" (Acts 8:36). That very same morning Seif telephoned Coralis and told her that they had struck water at sixty-one meters! "How great is the Lord!" Coralis thought. God had heard the pleas of the *mamas*, Coralis, and Susan.

During Ramadhan in October 2008, Susan arrived in Mombasa to visit the well. With Seif, they once again traveled up to Shimba Hills and were greeted by joyful villagers who were dancing and singing. The women thought the fresh-flowing water tasted sweet. Life has definitely improved in the village since the well was built. Young girls attend school instead of trekking down the mountain to draw water from the river, and there are no more deaths from crocodiles. There are also fewer water-borne diseases. Even the goats produce more milk. Coralis sums it all up: "The Lord listens to the cry of the poor," she says.

(Coralis Salvador)

Susan being draped in a kanga at the
celebration of the completed well.

This part of Coralis's ministry came to an abrupt halt in January 2009 when Coralis was fired from the rescue center. Part of her responsibilities as the human resource person for the Maryknoll Lay Missioners had been to mentor any new lay missioners who arrived and walk with them in their first year of mission. So she had traveled to Nairobi to welcome them and provide an orientation program for three new lay missioners assigned to Kenya. Prior to the formal orientation, an administrator of her organization had asked to meet with her. Given her usual up-beat spirit, she thought the meeting was to discuss the orientation program. Her mind imploded when she was told that her services were no longer required at the rescue center. An official of the FBO, in conjunction with the superior of the order of nuns assigned to the rescue center, had planned Coralis's abrupt exit with no advance warning or discussion with her. The reasons given seemed very sketchy, but one thing was very sure: the sisters wanted Coralis out of the center immediately.

On the surface she was told that her presence in the center was "in conflict" with how the sisters wanted to operate the center. Now that the center's programs were up and running, the nuns didn't want to be questioned or second guessed by Coralis. Instead, they expected obedience from her. Coralis had questioned them about many things, including the need for proper accounting procedures and the preferential treatment the sisters had been showing to some members of the staff. They added that Coralis had repeatedly violated a cultural norm, in taking over both the building of the water well and the rescue center. She was too intimidating. She was not supposed to tell the sisters, or the corrupt development director or water engineer, that something was wrong, that there were problems. She was expected to be more circumspect. The subtext of the workings of the institutional churches and the religious order were also in play: obey and do not question authority. Her Western mentality clashed dramatically with her adopted culture, even after all these years as a missioner.

Coralis was instructed to go quietly and that any dialogue with the sisters would be futile. Coralis was in shock, angry, and overcome with tears. She has been fired from the rescue center that she had given birth to, and with no discussion or warning. "How could this be? I gave it all my effort and all my love. I felt bereft and betrayed." She prayed for strength and focus to proceed with the orientation meeting. She put aside hurt emotions and anger, and began the program. That evening, with no one to turn to, she cried her heart out until early morning. At 6:00 in the morning, she awoke with a burning urge to attend the 6:15 mass. Half awake, still feeling the pangs of hurt and without showering, she half-heartedly dragged herself to the chapel across the courtyard from her room.

To her amazement and surprise, Coralis heard her Lord speak to her through the reading of the day. "God is not unfair. He will not forget the work you did or the love you showed for him in the help you gave and are still giving to your fellowmen. Our great desire is that each one of you keep up [his/her] eagerness to the end so that the things you hope for will come true" (Hebrews 6:11). Coralis left the chapel that morning imbued with God's spirit of understanding and love. She made it through the day and returned to Mombasa with the hope that a new door would open.

What did Coralis learn from this emotionally painful incident? It was that pride will get you every time! She had been involved in five separate programs at once: the AIDS Orphans' Project, the epilepsy clinic, the school for the deaf, the Shimba Hills well, and the rescue center. She should have done a better job of sharing authority. She could have nudged others and been less in your face. To this day, she is unsure of what the local people, her colleagues, or others thought of her dismissal. She continued work with her orphans, and no one ever spoke of it again. That is the Kenyan way. She has forgiven all involved, but like the scar from a wound, many years later, although the pain has ebbed, there is still an ache.

Chapter 6

Blessed Are Those
Who Are Poor but Have Dignity

The Voluntary Testing and
Counseling Clinic (VCT)

John Mullen, a Maryknoll Brother and nurse originally from Massachusetts, served in Kenya for twenty years, and worked in Mombasa for the last fourteen years. In 1996 he had established the Community Based Health Care (CBHC) program, the first HIV/AIDS outreach facility in Bomu, Mombasa. It currently serves four thousand people from all religious traditions. Over six feet tall, John had a large presence. He wore oversized horn-rimmed glasses, spoke in a loud baritone voice, and loved Italian food. As a missioner, he was intense, passionate, funny, and he worked tirelessly. He also served as a mentor to Coralis, and she watched, listened, and followed his every action. In the early days of her ministry, John assigned Juliana, a social worker at CBHC, to Coralis with the instruction to "make Coralis a social worker." Unfortunately, John passed away suddenly in April of 2010 due to poor health, yet his legacy looms large in Mombasa. Coralis says, "I will always be grateful to John for his life, his friendship, and his mentoring. He showed me the true meaning of dying to oneself, a letting go of me to be totally in service to others."

CBHC's main headquarters is in the VCT clinic in the Mikindani area of Mombasa. The VCT clinic is the nerve center for all HIV-related outreach to combat the pandemic. Coralis was spending two days a week in the VCT office. The clinic is set back off of a dusty, congested road in a large two-story building. It is next to a vocational school that some of the AIDS orphans attend. Over the years, the clinic has added eleven subclinics throughout the various slums of Mombasa. VCT is a well-known acronym that is magnified on many billboards throughout Kenya. This is where people go for testing, counseling, diagnosis, and treatment related to HIV/AIDS.

The clinic is always abuzz with activity. This is where life's tragedies and hopes play out daily. The outside courtyard is lush with verdant natural foliage. Hanging on trees, male weaver birds build hanging nests in the shape of small pouches. Chickens and goats mill about, and occasionally hawks swoop down to nab a chick. Patients are everywhere, with some waiting their turn in long lines flowing outside the building and others undecided about entering.

Inside the clinic, many men, women, children, and *mamas* with babies in their arms or slung to their backs sit patiently waiting their turn. Many young children dart around playing, oblivious to where they are; others, who are too weak to stand, lie on the floor. Various sisters, health-care workers, physicians, pharmacists, nurses, counselors, and social workers tend to the patients. In spite of the seriousness of AIDS, everyone appears relaxed. It is impossible to tell what is going on in the minds of these patients and their families. What is the status of the infants, the children, the *mamas*?

The steady stream of people going up and down the central staircase is similar to the chaotic flow in a busy subway station. Everyone waiting in the treatment and pharmacy area is sick, young and old alike, but people sit patiently on long wooden benches waiting their turn. There is no chit-chat, no cooing over a baby. This is serious business, and the mood is somber.

Coralis shares an office on the second floor with the IT staff. Hundreds of patient charts are jammed on desks and stacked on the floor, stools, and shelves. Coralis consults with the social workers in arranging support for all the orphans and guardians. She meets with potential new orphans, explains the entry criteria to those attempting to enter the Orphans' Project, and sets up home visits.

"The hardest part of my job is when I have to turn down a child for the program. Over half of the children I see are not eligible. They may be orphaned but not because of HIV/AIDS. Then there are some adults who come in with children from up country claiming guardianship. This has to be investigated and proven. In many instances, people have been referred by imams, village chiefs, or priests, but if they are not AIDS-related, I must refer these desperate people to other organizations. I usually write an introductory note for them to try to ease their entry into an appropriate program. Other times we have simply run out of money."

"It hurts not to be able to help," she sighs. "It's disappointing. Every time I go to the clinic, I know that for some people I can only offer my ears. All I can do is listen to them. Then when they leave, I take a deep breath, say a brief prayer, make my notes, and go on to welcome the next patient."

The Generation of HIV/AIDS Youths

Lucy Nyaga, a registered nurse and pediatric counselor, works in tandem with Coralis. Lucy is a petite woman who bubbles with joyful energy. How does Lucy keep her spirits up when she is surrounded by such sadness and despair? Lucy responds, "There is a time to suffer and a time to be blessed in life. Where others see despair, I see hope and blessings. It's rewarding to witness hope that was once lost restored—to see the patients gain courage after counseling to accept their status and to live positively. AIDS is no longer a death sentence or a disease just for prostitutes." Lucy said that her families, both Christian and Muslim, have great faith. "I never look back. I always look from the current situation to a positive future. I always focus to the front, not backward. We accept the situation and move forward, trusting that God is always with us in the good and the bad."

When Coralis began her mission work in 2001, the vast majority of HIV-positive infants and children died quickly. In 2004, after the availability of free antiretroviral drugs (ARVs) for children, they began to live longer and have a greater capacity for a full life. In the beginning, it was necessary to address the psychosocial needs of these HIV-positive children. One of the biggest challenges was telling them of their status. Lucy and the support staff implemented programs to counsel and disclose their status to the children. "We gathered them together in separate support groups according to their age. We have the 'Kid's Club' for children from three to eight years of age. These kids are not yet ready to be told their status. They are given some other reason for their need to take the drugs (ARVs). The

'Junior Teens' group are from eight to twelve years of age. They are told their status, receive group counseling, and are trained to take their meds independent of their parents or guardians. They are also taught how AIDS is spread. The last group is the 'Senior Teens,' ages thirteen to eighteen. We teach them about safe sex. They are typical teenagers in one sense, but with their HIV-positive status, they can be very bitter toward their parents, themselves, and others. All these children can be emotionally fragile."

In March 2010, during Susan's third visit to Mombasa, she and Coralis attended support groups for the junior and senior teens. They traveled to Mbungoni, north of Mombasa, to meet the junior group. Esther, a nurse and widowed single parent of a young son, met them in an outside alcove of an adjacent church. Strikingly beautiful and smartly dressed, with a gentle mannerism, Esther worked closely with Coralis to identify and monitor the project's orphans. Esther explained that this was only the second meeting of this junior teen group. A goal was to get the teens to be self-sufficient in taking their meds. Since many of the kids were orphans themselves, living with extended family members or guardians, often they were not the family's first priority. To further complicate matters, sometimes their guardians were undependable drug addicts or alcoholics.

One by one the children came straggling in over a period of about a half hour, some with a mother or guardian and some with an older sibling, but none looked happy. There were only seven or eight in the group at this time, but within a year it would grow to over twenty-five junior teens. They were all small for their ages. Esther and Coralis talked with the kids in Swahili. When Susan asked if they believed in God, Winnie, eleven years old, began to cry. She didn't understand Susan's question. She said she wanted to change her name because when her father died from AIDS, his family came and threw them out of their shanty. Her mother had also died from AIDS. This child was so very fragile, so they held her close, trying to comfort her. Esther promised to follow up with her guardian.

Nzomba, a small twelve-year-old AIDS orphan, said that when he takes his meds, he prays to God to make him well so he can finish school and someday become a lawyer. Speaking casually yet with conviction, he said, "I feel good about taking my meds because they will help me live longer." Another girl said she "forgets" to take her meds. Esther made a note of this and planned to follow up with the guardian. The hope is that in time the group will gel and become supportive to one another.

A few days later, they met with the senior teen group in a large brightly lit community room on the second floor of the clinic. About twenty-five teens came streaming in after school, giggling, laughing, and greeting friends. The staff doctor, counselors, and social workers welcomed them, and they seemed to have an easy rapport with each other. The kids headed straight over to a health worker, seated by a huge grey plastic container, the size of a large drum. The woman dipped a red plastic mug into the drum, filled it with an off-white porridge-like substance and handed it to the kids who drank it like soda. It was a fortified food supplement donated by the Church of Jesus Christ of the Latter-day Saints (the Mormon Church). The kids called it *Uji wa Jesu* (Jesus porridge). For some, it would be the only food they would have all day. Dressed in jeans and t-shirts, they took their seats in two semicircle rows. The Muslim girls all wore *hijab* (a veil). The kids in this group were also physically small for their ages.

Since the group was most comfortable in Swahili, Coralis and Margaret, the counselor, translated. No one was shy, and they all seemed eager to be heard. Susan asked about God, fairness, and AIDS. They were surprised by the questions. Their reaction was like, "How can Susan not know the answers to this stuff?" In a teachable moment, many teenagers were eager to come up front to speak and enlighten Susan. Each one basically told her that all they had to do was take the drugs and they would be fine. But if you decided not to take the drugs, you would die. It was cut and dry. No big deal for them. They believed their illness was no different from any other chronic disease like diabetes, malaria, or tuberculosis. This was a group of joyful but chronically ill kids who accepted and saw a future filled with possibilities. Many had been chosen to be mentors to kids in the junior teen group. They were able to share their experiences about drug awareness, self-acceptance, and the importance of attending the support group. The seniors feel proud to be asked to be a mentor; the juniors feel accepted by the seniors, which gives them hope.

What is the difference between the junior and senior groups? The juniors had just been told that they were HIV positive. It will take them time to adjust their thinking and to understand the implications of their condition. The seniors who had already gone through this process were emboldened HIV-positive kids who embraced Lucy's philosophy of "accept and move forward."

Sometimes not all the children "get it" at the same time. For Coralis, even though all her orphans were equal, some were more equal. Orphan Beverly is one such child. She and her sister Lily are HIV positive and entered the program after their mother died of AIDS. At the time Beverly was ten, and Lily was eight. They have three siblings, and their eldest brother acts as their guardian. When Beverly was in Class 8, the project was able to send her to a secondary boarding school. Coralis made sure that the school was near a clinic that dispensed the ARVs. In the beginning, Beverly went to the clinic and took her medications daily. When questioned by her classmates, she just told them that she was praying with the sisters. But then, without telling anyone, she soon stopped taking the ARVs because she was "feeling better." At the end of the term, Beverly's blood tests at the VCT revealed she had stopped the medications.

"Lucy and I realized that sending Beverly to a boarding school was not a good idea. She was not emotionally ready and still required close monitoring. She failed Form 1 and enrolled in a nearby secondary day school to repeat the year. The VCT staff got her back on her medications, but her school performance did not really improve. But the staff would not give up on Beverly, and she would not give up on herself." In an unusual move, Coralis allowed her to repeat Form 1 once again. "We give extra attention and leeway to the AIDS orphans. These kids have a lot to deal with besides just being orphans. Because of their health, we let them stay in the program longer than orphans who are not HIV positive. To me, it just seems fair because they innocently came into this world with AIDS. We want to be able to give them as much opportunity as possible." Beverly has now moved onto Form 2 and gets extra help in math; she takes her meds regularly and has a very inquisitive mind.

Benson and Victor, both HIV-positive orphans, are the first HIV-positive kids in the project to finish secondary school. They participated in the VCT junior and senior teen support groups, and they were part of the Education for Life and Adventures Unlimited workshops. Coralis beams like a proud mother knowing that these young men have succeeded. "A decade ago, when I first began mission work, HIV-positive children were dead by the age of five. In Victor and Benson, I see a generation of HIV-positive kids who are not only living but making something out of their lives. Both of these boys persevered. The project gave them the opportunity, but they themselves were the 'poor but hardworking' and 'poor but determined.'" Benson is currently awaiting his results in the national exam and is thinking about becoming a doctor.

Is There Hope for a Generation Born Free of AIDS?

Coralis shared office space in Chamgamwe with a number of CBHC nurses over the years. They administer the HIV/AIDS tests, monitor patients, and dispense medications. Marion Wakesho, a tall, attractive nurse in her mid-thirties, is very energetic. She and Coralis developed an easy collegial relationship. Marion is married, with one child, and her husband is never sure how many orphans she will bring home on a given day. They provide them with temporary shelter until a permanent placement can be found. Marion has yet to convince her husband to adopt one of the orphans, but she never stops trying.

Marion admits that her greatest challenge is the "inability to deal with all their needs and basic wants due to the limited resources such as food, adequate housing, and higher education." Often times, she will burst into Coralis's office pleading passionately, "You have to help this orphan! You need to help this teenager! Take this child to the rescue center!" "I try to calm her down and take a more tempered approach," says Coralis.

Marion discovered Sarafina, a destitute seven-year-old girl who was not an orphan nor HIV positive in Bogobogoni, a Changamwe slum. As Marion examined her, she was horrified to discover cigarette burn marks all over her malnourished body. Marion learned that Sarafina had been abused by her uncle. She found Sarafina's mother who told her that she and Sarafina had run away from her abusive husband. "I was able to give the child food and counsel the mother, but other than that, there was not much more I could do," says Coralis. Sarafina did not fall within the project's parameters. A short time later, the family simply disappeared. In her desire to help, Marion never stopped trying to bring cases to Coralis.

Preventing HIV-positive pregnant mothers from transmitting the disease to their newborns is the focus of another CBHC program. The Preventing Mother-to-Child Transmission (PMTCT) programs in Africa are sponsored by UNICEF, the World Health Organization, and other nongovernmental organizations (NGOs). Mother-to-child transmission occurs when an HIV-positive mother passes the virus to her baby. This can occur during delivery and also by breast-feeding. Without treatment, around 15 to 30 percent of the babies born to HIV-positive mothers will become infected with HIV during delivery. A further 5 to 20 percent become infected due to breast-feeding.

CBHC health workers from the community attempt to identify any women who might be pregnant and then to educate them to ensure that the disease will not be transmitted to the newborn. Most consent to participate in the program. Other mothers have lingering fears of side effects or hold on to antiquated beliefs that a curse or evil spirit will harm their child. Generally, if the pregnant woman has a male partner living with her, they are both educated about PMTCT. The husband or partner is asked to support the program to ensure that the outcome is successful. Coralis has witnessed the success of this program for a number of her guardians. These women give birth to HIV-negative children and are no longer in fear that they will transmit the disease through breast-feeding.

Susan asked Lucy if she could realistically foresee a time when there would be a generation of Kenyans without AIDS. She smiled, "Not this generation. But I see the programs working. I see the youths becoming empowered. It takes time. Yes, it will happen, God willing."

AIDS Orphans to the University

Technically, when the youths in the program complete Form 4 of high school, the project has no further responsibility to support them. Coralis speaks softly about this, her voice pausing to handle her overflowing emotion. "My orphans have been with me for many years. They are like my own children. I have all their photos from the time they entered. I have seen them grow into adulthood. It's difficult to let them go. When they are eligible for college scholarships, I cannot allow their dreams to be broken due to lack of money. They worked so hard, studying, applying themselves, staying focused."

Maurice Ochieng, twenty-two years old, is one such orphan. His father died from AIDS in 1997. His HIV-positive mother is the sole breadwinner for her eight children and sells cooked food to support her family. Maurice was a consistent "A" student from primary through secondary school and scored an "A" on the national exam. The project has supported him, plus his three siblings, from primary school on.

Maurice is a very serious and shy young man. He is a tall, thin, dark-skinned African with a broad engaging smile. Susan asked him about his belief in God? Did he wonder if God was there for poor people? "When I was sixteen years old, I knew there were so many problems in my home. My father died. My mother couldn't pay our school fees. It was then I knew that I was different from other kids. I had to do something to put food on the table. Yes, I have wondered where God is. Why are there social classes? Why is the gap between the rich and poor increasing at a higher rate? I wonder if God knows why this is happening. I was first mad at God when I saw my friends being better off than me in terms of materialistic things. I got over that through prayer and asked God to provide for me, close the gap between me and my friends, and it happened."

What does blessed are the poor mean for Maurice? "I think it is in terms of humility and meekness. The poor consider themselves so lowly. They usually surrender their life to God in order for God to help them. In this way God is considering them and blessing them." When Susan asked what part hope plays in the blessing, he responded, "Hope is having the expectation to achieve certain goals in your

Coralis with Maurice Ochieng and Joseph Mwanake, two orphans now doing university studies in Nairobi.

life. I feel a responsibility to my brothers and sisters to ensure that they take their studies seriously because education is the only option available to take them out of the prevailing economic hardship."

This quiet, studious young man then turned to Coralis and spoke, "I thank God for bringing Mama Coralis into my life at a time when I had lost hope. She restored my confidence in my studies and I thank God for this." Maurice is currently in his second year at a university in Nairobi and is doing well academically in an engineering program. His scholarship pays for his tuition, but he is responsible for his board and all other expenses. He perseveres despite the financial hardship with everlasting hope and faith in God.

Tabitha Wangari, eighteen years old, is one of five children. Her father died in 2000, and her mother, who is HIV positive, sells homemade soap and vegetables for a living. One brother is HIV positive, and her sister died from AIDS. Their mother is also guardian of a seven-year-old HIV-positive nephew, the child of her deceased sister. The family lives in a shanty they built themselves out of sisal poles and mud. Initially, the roof was thatched but it did not keep out the heavy rains. Tabitha's mother saved money to buy iron sheets for a new roof.

Tabitha, a petite, mature young woman with a warm and comfortable smile, required emergency assistance in 2008 and entered the project. Her mother could not raise the school fees and materials necessary to continue her schooling. Tabitha is an excellent student, serious and committed to her studies. She carries herself confidently and always maintains a faith-filled attitude. When Susan met her in March 2010, she had just learned her scores on the national secondary school exam. She scored highest in the entire Changamwe region and knew that she qualified for a university scholarship. "I would like to be an electrical engineer when I go to the university next year. I have loved math since I was a kid. I later developed a passion for physics and electronics. I want to have a good job so that I can help my family out of poverty. Kenya, as a developing nation, needs more engineers who are competitive in order to help our nation move toward achieving our goals. I think I can help make a change, even if small, to help our country move forward."

What role does faith play in Tabitha's life? "I see poverty all around me: people who lack the basic needs of food and clothing. I wonder why God allows some people to suffer so and have these needs. I pray to God as I wonder why there is such a big gap between the rich and the poor. Some people have all the things they need, and others do not. I ask why God allows these things to happen. I think that God wants me to go through this process in life so I can understand life and its challenges so that I will know that life is not easy. It's all about struggling."

What does blessed are the poor mean for Tabitha? "This means blessed are the poor who have faith in their hearts. God has blessed us [but] not in material things. Some people believe they are righteous and closer to God than other people. These are the hypocrites. But the truly blessed poor are those who do not take themselves to be very righteous. They are close to God. They are not hypocrites." Susan asked if she worries about her future. "I don't feel bad for myself that I am an AIDS orphan. I focus on my future and what will become of me in five to ten years. What will my life be like? This is what makes me work harder. My faith teaches me that the first shall become last and the last shall become first. I believe that one day I will come out of poverty and have a better life."

In February 2011, Kenyan universities posted their student acceptances. Tabitha gained admission to four universities in Nairobi, and they offered her a scholarship for tuition. She still has to find a way to pay for her board and other fees.

In the end, the journey simply goes back to faith. In the words of theologian Albert Nolan,

> It is a particular kind of conviction that something can and will happen because it is good and because it is true that goodness can and will triumph over evil. In other words it is the conviction that God is good to humanity and that God can and will triumph over all evil. The power of faith is the power of goodness and truth, which is the power of God.[1]

The Kingdom of God and Living in the Presence

> Do not conform yourselves to the standards of this world, but let God transform you inwardly by a complete change of your mind. Then you will be able to know the will of God—what is good and is pleasing to God and is perfect. (Romans 12:2)

In mission life, Coralis spent much time in prayerful meditation, and the past decade culminated in a much deeper union with her God. "The kingdom of God is the fruit of living in the presence. It is an attitude of trust and

---

[1]   Nolan, *Jesus before Christianity*, 39.

Tabitha Wangari, studying at Kenyatta University in Nai-
robi and a volunteer with the AIDS Orphans Project.

loving attention to God, who is in us and around us. Every selfless act of charity and solidarity with the poor brings God's love alive to them. When we become the hands of God, our acts bring about empowerment and their lives are changed. Our lives are changed also as the marginalized poor become missioners to those of us who serve them. Only when poverty is eradicated in its entirety, will the kingdom of God be fully realized."

Coralis wrote almost forty quarterly newsletters during her mission life. They were intended to bridge the informational gap between what was happening on the ground in Kenya and the people back home. Writing these reports certainly wasn't her favorite job. She procrastinated, but she knew she had deadlines to meet and money to raise for her orphans. Coralis maintained a habit of keeping a journal of personal reflections and quotes from theological and spiritual readings. Prominent in the reports—not by the word count in the text, but surely by the impact of the passage—were selections by authors she relied upon for spiritual sustenance: Dorothy Day, Dallas Willard, Joan Chittister, Flannery O'Connor, Phillip Brooks, Frederick Buechner, Ibn al-Arabi, Dietrich Bonhoeffer, Bede Griffiths, C. S. Lewis, and G. K. Chesterton, as well as Scripture passages from Romans, Hebrews, and John. A favorite passage from Scriptures is "Do not let your heart be troubled. You have faith in God" (John 14:1). These journal entries would eventually make their way into her newsletters, each of which required an entire day of reflection and writing.

In the great majority of these reports, Coralis shared her thoughts about the kingdom of God. "Being in mission gave me daily opportunities to experience the kingdom of God, to be living in the presence, for the people that you

serve, and unknowingly, for your own spiritual development. I believe that whenever we show care and give hope
and love to another as God's partner in the here and now,
we bring about the kingdom."

The Dying Man of Maumba

During Holy Week, between Palm Sunday and Easter
Sunday 2002, Coralis found herself as the designated driver
for Father Joe in Mivumoni. He had had a truck accident
and although unhurt, his vehicle had been badly damaged.
Nonetheless, he was expected to perform the rites for his
entire parish during the busiest season of the liturgical year,
which included Holy Thursday, Good Friday, the Easter
Vigil, and Easter Sunday. The parish itself incorporates seven
substations in the vast geographic area of Kenya's Shimba
Hills. Since Coralis was the only person who had a car, Joe
asked her to drive him on his pastoral rounds.

Coralis describes what for her was an experience of the
reign of God. "From Palm Sunday to Easter Sunday, I felt
like a priest doing all the services. The Dima outstation is
more than a one and a half hour drive from Mivumoni
through rugged terrain. The other stations are about twenty
to forty-five minutes apart. Unfortunately this was during
the long rainy season, so we drove through torrential rain,
mud, rivers of water and sand, as we climbed up and down
endless hills and through forests and fields. The weather
was oppressively hot and humid. I felt like a rally car driver
enduring all kinds of road hurdles. The scariest moment was
driving from Majimboni at night. It was pitch black and I
had to maneuver through a river of sand. Joe was teaching
me how to maneuver the vehicle by calling out instructions

beside me. With my heart pounding, my body sweating, and my eyes riveted, I could barely control the car. It pivoted like a pendulum, left then right, deluging the windshield with new layers of rain and mud. Throughout all of this, I had to maintain a steady speed and a straight course in order that we wouldn't sink.

"After four masses on Holy Saturday and four more on Easter Sunday, all in different locations, we were physically exhausted when we were asked to visit Patrick, a fifty-year-old man who was dying of AIDS. We found him lying on a mat under a mango tree next to his mud hut. He was covered with a sheet except for his hands and face. Patrick had no family, but he was surrounded by the community who cared for him. They had swept the area free of dry leaves and debris to make him more comfortable. He looked old beyond his years, with thin, sunken eyes and long withered fingers. As his neighbors brought a stool for Joe, we all stood around Patrick. Joe bent low, huddled close to Patrick's ears. The only sound was the mumbling coming from Joe and Patrick. Then we all prayed together for his peaceful death. Later, as we were leaving, I looked back over my left shoulder and saw twenty or more villagers who encircled Patrick's mat, softly praying and singing hymns. Seeing the love extended to Patrick, that accompanied him as he passed from life to death, was an extraordinary spiritual moment. I was teary-eyed, but strangely enough, not for Patrick's dying. It was a joy for me to behold his peaceful death surrounded by a loving community.

"The amazing part of my Holy Week journey was the felt presence of God, especially on our way back to Mivumoni from visiting Patrick. For the last seven kilometers, the car seemed to glide over the gaping holes and boulders in the road. Somehow, this drive was effortless, unlike the previous day when we traveled that same road. That late Easter afternoon, with the sky turning a purple red toward dusk, I truly experienced God's presence."

The Two Women of Changamwe

Many people either infected or affected by AIDS visit Coralis's office in Changamwe. No one needs an appointment. One day in March 2010 two young women arrived seeking her help. Mweni, a single HIV-positive mother of one boy in Form 2, was brought by her neighbor Halima. Mweni was weak and tired, suffering from the side effects of the ARVs. Halima accompanied her because Mweni was too weak to come on her own. They came from the Kwa Jumvo side of the village of Miritini, west of Mombasa. They walked ten kilometers down steep hilly slopes because they did not have the fifteen shillings (twenty cents) for a *matatu*.

Coralis greeted them and came from behind her desk to be seated in a small circle with them. Halima, a mother of four young children ages two through ten, told Coralis that she had been beaten by her husband when he came home drunk. Both women poured out their problems to Coralis. The conversation, in Swahili, went on for over an hour. Susan was sitting off in a corner but could not understand what was being said. She knew however, that something very profound was taking place in front of her. Mweni, a teacher's aide in a private primary school, wanted assistance with private-school fees for her son. Her employer was late in paying her salary, and her son had been sent home from school because she could not pay his fees. Coralis asked why she didn't send him to a government school that would be cheaper, but Mweni responded that she believed that a private school could provide her boy with a better education. Halima asked for help for uniforms and shoes for her two children in primary school.

Coralis immediately knew that the AIDS Orphans' Project could not help either of them because they did not meet the program's criteria. Mweni's child was not an orphan, and Halima was married and her children were not orphans. But rather than just send them away, Coralis felt they needed someone to listen to them. "I had a sense that there was another story. I asked them how they managed in the past. How were they able to survive? Assuming their belief, I asked how God was present to them during their hard times. Looking back, they said that whenever they had problems, God was there for them, helping them. They realized that they solved their own problems. They could do it again. They were 'poor but determined,' 'poor but hard-working,' and 'poor but they had dignity.' When they left, I knew their spirits had been lifted, and my spirit was lifted for them. It was a holy moment for me because I knew they had regained the energy to help themselves. Even though I didn't give them anything material, their burden was lifted. I experienced God's presence in our sharing, and that presence imbued Mweni and Halima with a fire in their hearts. I was joyfully happy for them and ecstatic to share that moment with these women."

God's Grace Abounds

Grace is God's own life, shared by us and open to all. God's life is love and by grace we are able to share God's selfless love. It is everywhere, and it surrounds us with the energy of the Spirit. But it is up to us to respond to the gift of grace, to access it, to make it our own. Grace is part of our humanness whatever our religious, cultural, or ancestral beliefs.

In the African culture, it is difficult to draw the distinction between religion and culture. The two are inextricably intertwined. At the core, each African believes in God; there are no atheists. By the time a child is born, she/he is already imbued with certain religious and cultural systems, predetermined by the parents and ancestors. Life has a continuous pattern or rhythm; you are born, grow up, get old, and die. Life never comes to an end; rather, the person simply changes form. Is it possible that these religious, cultural, and ancestral beliefs contribute to the certitude of a better tomorrow?

The blessings for the AIDS orphans and others living in brutal poverty include a great degree of certainty and contentment amidst the chaos of their surroundings. Those who are poor but determined, hardworking, and truthful have an incredible sense of hope and even joy that they will survive; that despite food insecurity, they will have food; that despite the incredible yearning for the parental love they have lost, they will be cared for and overcome their circumstances; that even without the necessary fees for their education, they will be educated as a way to lift them out of the poverty.

For Westerners, all these challenges seem unbearable. Yet for the vast majority of individuals in this story, their blessings include the mind-set that the Lord will truly take care of them. They simply go on with their lives. They have God, Allah, and the ancestors, and they are able to rise above what to a Westerner would be the total despair of their circumstances. They have the hope, born out of their continuing faith, that they and their families will survive. Still, it's more than survival: it's the keeping together of the family unit. This connectedness with one another is their African tradition.

Whether Muslim or Christian, by incorporating their ancestral traditions, they say that God is there for them, "everyday, because we breathe, we walk, we see the day. . . . Then we are OK." While this may seem hard to believe for Westerners, it's in their makeup; surviving is part of their human nature. They say *Inshallah*, meaning "God willing." This describes their inner peace.

In their emptiness of material things and often without food, the poor are able to connect in an unencumbered way with a sense of true hope and joy. The burden of the poor is made lighter by their faith. This is their blessing.

Epilogue

"To Everything There Is a Season"

The summer of 2009 brought with it a profound change for Coralis as she returned home to San Francisco to witness the birth of her first grandchild. She was now *Shoshoo* (grandmother in Kikuyu, a Kenyan tribal language) to Preston. "I held the son of my firstborn child in my arms. I loved him in an instant. My missionary world was suspended for that month in California. My orphans, the grandmothers and guardians, the challenges and heartbreak of the slums were a distant haze. I was just *Shoshoo*."

After returning to Mombasa, she was torn between grandson Preston and the orphans. "This is one of the pains in following the call to mission. We live in uncertainty and on the edge, neither here nor there. Preston is blessed to grow up in an environment of love and in a society that values children. Our orphans live a life full of unimaginable challenges. The Kenyan government seems to do little to alleviate the suffering of the marginalized poor; instead, it relies on the NGOs to care for the people. Often I can't help but think that I am contributing to the government's irresponsibility. As I approach the end of my third contract, these are the questions I struggle with."

Once Coralis returned to Kenya in 2010, she spent the better part of the next year trying to bond with Preston via Skype. Despite the ten-hour time difference, the baby's schedule, power outages, and Internet breakdowns, she managed to connect with him often before daybreak. Wanting to look her best, she dressed in bright colors and put on makeup. In the background, amplified by the surrounding mosques, the Muslim call to prayer could be heard.

When the screen lit up and Preston appeared, Coralis danced and sang to him. She moved to the beat of the music of her soul. As he grew from infant to toddler, he smiled broadly, joyful with glee, singing with her and reaching out to the screen to touch her. "Yes, Preston, *Shoshoo* is here. *Shoshoo* loves you," she cried out, seemingly reaching into the computer to connect with him. As Preston whirled around in his walker, her son, Paolo, followed with the Webcam. After each call, Coralis was left exhilarated, yet bereft with longing.

Again, Coralis endured the triannual discernment process. Should she renew her contract or call it quits after ten years of service? "As in the past, I simply waited for the Lord to give me a sign. It always happens the same way. I wait until the very end before I commit, but this time it was much harder. Another son, Pietro, and his wife told me they were expecting their first child in the summer of 2010. I have five children. I knew it wouldn't be long before other babies arrived, and I wanted to be part of all of their lives."

Coralis decided to take a one-year leave of absence. "I intended to take that time to rest, reflect, and ponder where God was calling me next. Mission life in Mombasa has been a life-giving adventure. I have attained a deeper union with my God. Being immersed in the lives of the sick and marginalized was truly living out my faith. But would this, could this continue outside of mission life?" She would not know the answer until she left Mombasa.

During this time, Susan was going through her own discernment struggle. This stage of her life had never been better. Her children were grown and independent. Her health was good, and she had completed nearly twenty-five very satisfying years practicing law. She applied to the Franciscan Mission Service (FMS) as a lay missioner because she was drawn to the Franciscan spirituality of prayer, community, simple living, and working hand in hand with the poor. In the fall of 2010 she began a thirteen-week formation process with the FMS in Washington, DC.

"A Time to Keep and a Time to Cast Away"

Before her leave of absence, Coralis anguished over who would take up her responsibilities at the AIDS Orphans' Project. Three new Maryknoll Lay Missioners arrived in Kenya in January 2010, and she was hopeful that one would feel the call to serve the AIDS orphans. Mary Oldham, a chemical engineer from Iowa, took up the challenge. "I was searching for how to live out my faith more fully," says Mary. "Originally I thought that meant getting involved in fair trade or other work outside of engineering. I researched international programs and connected with an American couple in Malawi. The very moment I read their blog, I knew I wanted to do what they were doing. I applied to Catholic Relief Service's volunteer program and went to Uganda for one year. I worked on a village microfinance project and loved it! When the program ended, I came back to the States and applied to the Maryknoll Lay Missionary program."

Mary moved into Coralis's flat in Mombasa and slowly became accustomed to the sweltering heat as well as her new assignment. Coralis gave her as much support as she could while preparing herself to leave Mombasa, perhaps permanently. Over the past decade, she had made deep friendships among her colleagues. She also found a rich source of friendship and support among the Muslims of Mombasa. She would be saying good-bye to Kizingo, the butcher and her source of meat and fish, who almost daily measured out her purchases in kilos and placed them in small plastic bags. Mohammed Awadh, the supplier of uniforms, shoes, and school bags had really helped her out by agreeing to bill her monthly. Her landlady, Hamida, thoughtfully advised Coralis not to hang her *choopies* (underwear) on the outside clothesline because it would be considered insulting to the Kenyans. Kassim, her car mechanic, had rescued her every time her creaky, old four-wheel-drive broke down. All of these people were important parts of her support system.

By June 2010, Coralis had given away all of her material possessions, including many clothes. She gave the keys to her flat to Mary, said her final good-bye, and headed home. Within days, her second grandson was born in San Francisco. She quickly became absorbed in the lives of all of her children and grandchildren. She allowed herself this precious time to rest and refresh her being. Of course, there were occasional e-mails back and forth to Mary, checking on the orphans and lending support. She was very pleased that Mary had secured a small grant for the project. The funds were used for career counseling and to build two study libraries.

Father Joe called regularly from Mombasa to ask when she would be returning. "I haven't made up my mind," was her usual reply. Joe would always respond, "Coralis, there is nothing to think about. Just get on the plane!"

Steve Jalango, one of the orphans, had been Coralis's trusted assistant. When Coralis turned the project over to Mary and returned home, she strongly endorsed Steve, urging Mary to utilize Steve's knowledge and enthusiasm while she became orientated in mission. Unfortunately, within the first year, it became evident to Mary that Steve was stealing from the project. Money given to him to pay for some of the orphans' school fees never made it to the schools. Steve had falsified receipts, but parents, guardians, and school officials alerted Mary that the fees had not been paid. In one instance, Mary gave Steve money to purchase a commode for a disabled orphan. Again, Steve provided Mary with a receipt even though he never bought the commode for the orphan. When confronted, Steve had great difficulty admitting what he had done.

Corruption of government officials and the police permeate the system. Since the colonial era and postindependence, many politicians have used their offices unjustly to acquire personal wealth. There is much evidence throughout Kenya (and other countries as well) of corruption, embezzlement of public funds, and land grabbing of millions of acres of prime real estate. There is little respect on the part of citizens for elected and appointed individuals. Most ordinary citizens accept that there is a failure of integrity and transparency on the part of leadership. In order to transcend this system that permeates society, Kenya needs truly transformational leadership.

Most would agree that what Steve did is stealing. But

this is a complex societal issue, and poverty often obscures moral choices. Steve lives in an environment where conversations about the need to bribe officials, even those with the least amount of power, are accepted. A common expression is *kitu kidogo*, meaning "a little something," a small bribe, is needed. When Coralis was told about Steve's conduct, she felt terrible: "I was betrayed. I believed he had risen above the temptations of his environment. I feel sad because he was doing so well. His integrity seemed so far different than that of many others. But to have him betray not only Mary and myself, but also the orphans, makes me wonder if by trusting him with financial responsibilities, I may have contributed to his temptation."

In the spring of 2011, Coralis informed the Maryknoll Lay Missioners that she planned to return to Kenya to work on issues of child trafficking in a new program under development in Nairobi and Mombasa. "I went to mission for a selfish reason: to be more closely united with my God by serving and walking with the marginalized poor of Kenya. My years in Africa proved an adventure that, surprisingly, freed me from worldly cares and burdens. I lived in a daily spiritual paradox of 'detached attachment,' fully dependent on my Lord. After ten years, I chose to take time off to reconnect with my family. I wanted to see where I was being led and to experience the strength of my union with God in solidarity with the poor outside the context of mission. I discovered that I am not yet ready for a new adventure in the United States. I believe that I'm called to reembrace the challenge of mission. I missed the particular experience of God's presence that comes with life in mission. I return to Kenya with the hope of being recharged. I return to taste, to sense, to touch my God."

Ironically, Susan was assigned to the Justice, Peace and Integrity of Creation Franciscans Africa (JPICFA) office in Nairobi. The Franciscan Mission Service tries to partner with JPIC offices around the world. Susan's experience as an attorney and advocate for human rights will further equip the JPICFA office to assist those living in poverty and infected by HIV/AIDS and other diseases as well as refugees and displaced people fleeing drought, famine, and civil war.

Coralis returned to mission in August 2011 a few weeks after the birth of her first granddaughter. Susan followed at year's end after the birth of her first grandchild.

"A Time to Pluck Up That Which Is Planted"

In clear and unmistakable language, the Hebrew prophets, Mohammed, and Christ challenged people to change. We have the tools and resources to reduce the poverty and suffering of the poor. The impediment, says Franciscan Richard Rohr, a global leader in spiritual awakening, is the law of inertia. It is the tendency of a body to resist change or acceleration.

> [There] is the spiritual form of the law of inertia. Humans prefer what we are accustomed to; we want to go with the prevailing flow, the conveyor belt. Society and church are needed and wanted security systems, status symbols, wealth and warfare. . . . Social need and cultural inertia primarily determine much of people's morality.[1]

---

[1] Richard Rohr, *The Naked Now: Learning to See as the Mystics See* (New York: Crossroad Publishing, 2009), 95.

There is continued criticism within our own country about sending American foreign aid to developing countries when there is much poverty here in the United States. This is a legitimate criticism. However, what makes sense to Susan and Coralis is that poverty exists all over the world. If you are lucky enough to find a place that touches your soul, then you go. It's that simple, and Susan and Coralis found that place in Kenya. Opening ourselves up to new possibilities and experiences through our outreach to the poor, even for a short period of time, has immeasurable rewards. We are transformed not only by these people but by the natural beauty of the African landscape. In mission and service, we attain a spirit of detachment and become free to abandon what does not serve God's kingdom.

"A Time to Keep Silence and a Time to Speak"

When given the opportunity, many of the AIDS orphans use their lives to make a difference. They want to succeed and assist their extended family. This is part of the African spiritual way of living. They are connected to their ancestors, and their culture, ancestry, heritage, and knowledge constitutes the spiritual universe of their African consciousness.

Many of the orphans spoke of their poverty as a challenge to overcome. As Collins said, "Poverty gives me a determination to move forward. It inspires me and gives me hope. It also plays a major role in blessing my community because if I see someone without food, I am supposed to give him a hand. By helping that person get food or shelter, I will be blessed."

Joseph, the community activist who had become addicted to drugs in high school, is determined to use his poverty to make a difference. His project, "Sons of Mama Africa," helps drug addicts kick the habit. "I saw poverty from a very early age and have lived with it all my life. It pains me to see my people living in horrible conditions but something tells me I will turn this poverty around. There is a just God because he does not give you more than you can handle. We cannot be like people from the West because they have their way of life and we have ours. But we have time, and some of us are still learning and some of us are still crying. We have to feel this way and then we know God is there."

Zainabu, who was determined not to fall into prostitution, has also focused her efforts on community activism. "I believe God is there because he has taken me from where I did not know what would happen to me. I worried that I would get HIV because I might have to go around sleeping with men just to get money. But that did not happen to me. Now I appreciate everything I have. No, I will not sell myself!" Zainabu was recently trained to deliver health messages such as AIDS prevention through play acting and street theater. Her drama group is hoping to get funding from local sources to put on plays to teach about health in schools. In addition, she has been accepted at the Kenya Medical Training College in Nairobi where she will study community nursing. "As a Muslim, I believe the poor are blessed because God is testing our faith. Rich people sometimes do not even remember that God is there. At times I felt alone and wondered what my parents did to cause me to suffer. But now I believe I will be someone very important and that keeps me going."

Tabitha, who scored the highest in the Changamwe region on the national exam, volunteered to assist Mary in the AIDS Orphans' Project. She will also be attending Kenyatta University in Nairobi, studying for a bachelor's degree in health services management. Like the other orphans, she is determined to succeed. One of Tabitha's best friends in the AIDS Orphans' Project was Esha, the young Muslim girl who died in childbirth. "Esha was like me," says Tabitha. "We didn't feel bad that we were AIDS orphans." They felt lucky to be in the project since many AIDS orphans are abandoned and left to fend for themselves. Tabitha said that Esha finally felt that she had a life; she hadn't felt that way since her mother died.

Despite being conflicted about which religion to practice, Islam or Christianity, Esha had an abiding faith in God. "I pray for this poverty to end and to have a peaceful life. Those who are rich are supposed to assist those who are poor. If you are rich with material things and see your neighbor suffering, then you must assist that neighbor by any means possible." Although Esha's voice was silenced by her tragic death, we can hope that her daughter inherits her mother's will and determination to succeed and that her ancestral family will continue to surround and nourish her as she grows.

"A Time to Every Purpose Under Heaven"

In the African culture, life comes from God and returns to God. It is the Divine that has given life to the family, to the African lineage. The family, a concept far beyond the father and mother, is supposed to carry on life in this environment God has created. The African culture is alive and strong, especially in times of crisis. The AIDS orphans, their grandmothers and guardians, the social workers, health-care professionals, missioners, and many others daily embrace this cultural norm. The very fact that few of Coralis's orphans had to be placed in children's homes or orphanages demonstrates the importance given to family. Rarely can an individual survive outside the family, nor can the family survive outside the community.

We have experienced how these marginalized poor are truly blessed. In their material emptiness, they possess a liberating presence through their mind-set of hope and spirituality linked with their family, their community, the ancestors, and the world about them. Even the loss of parental love and an uncertain future cannot dampen their spirits.

The beatitude "blessed are the poor" is followed by the countervailing admonition, "But woe unto you that are rich for you have received your consolation" (Luke 6:24). Perhaps when we have much, we can be deluded into thinking that we have earned it, that we can thank ourselves for it. We lose any sense of spiritual poverty, the sense of dependence and total openness to the Divine. The message of the crucified poor, the suffering poor, the marginalized poor is that they do not put their trust in what is transitory. Only by being able to surpass ourselves, to let go of our possessive nature, can we discover this liberating presence that invites us to fully become our true selves and the knowledge that our personal spiritual well-being relies on our relationships with others. This is God's kingdom bearing the fruit of joy and unconditional love.

Blessed are the poor, for theirs is the kingdom of God. (Luke 6:20)